# WHO SAID THAT?

# WHO SAID THAT?

*Quotations and potted biographies of famous people*

Selected and compiled by

## Renie Gee

BOOK CLUB ASSOCIATES
London

This edition published 1984 by
Book Club Associates
By arrangement with David & Charles Ltd

First published as *Who Said That?* (1980), *More of Who Said That?*
(1981) and *Still More of Who Said That?* (1983)

# Introduction

When *Who Said That?* was first published, it raised many questions. Why, people asked, did you not include some of the best pieces by Dorothy Parker, Thomas Hardy, or W. H. Davies the Supertramp? Two more books were published to include all my friends' suggestions, such as a few French authors, present-day writers and those tried and true pieces we all learnt at school. This edition is a compilation of the three books, bringing all those quotations together in one handy volume.

It is a 'fun' book, aimed at giving the reader pleasure – a book which can be picked up in an idle moment and looked through with interest and amusement. If you find your favourite quotation here, that surely is added delight.

# Aesop

Beware lest you lose the substance by grasping at the shadow.

*Fables*

The gods help them that help themselves.

*Fables*

It is not only fine feathers that make fine birds.

*Fables*

Don't count your chickens before they are hatched.

*Fables*

Aesop (c550BC), a fabulist of antiquity, is said by Herodotus to have lived in the reign of Amasis of Egypt. Originally a slave, he is represented in later art as deformed, but he received his freedom and travelled as far afield as Greece.

# Joseph Addison

There was a Club of Fat Men that did not come together to entertain one another with Sprightliness and Wit, but to keep one another in Countenance.
The room where the Club met was something of the largest and had two Entrances, one by a Door of moderate Size and the other by a pair of Folding Doors. If a Candidate for this Corpulent Club could make his Entrance through the first he was looked upon as unqualified...
... if he stuck in the Passage and could not force his way through it, the Folding Doors were thrown open for his Reception, and he was saluted as a Brother.

In opposition to this Society there sprung up another, composed of Scare-Crows and Skeletons...
...At length they come to this Accommodation, that the two Bailiffs of the Town should be annually chosen out of the two Clubs; by which the principal Magistrates are at this Day coupled like Rabbets, one fat and one lean.

*On Clubs, The Spectator*

Joseph Addison (1672–1719) was a British essayist and poet. Born in Wiltshire, he was granted a pension to enable him to qualify for the Diplomatic Service by foreign travel, and in 1704 he celebrated Marlborough's victory at Blenheim in his poem *The Campaign*. He became Under-Secretary of State, Secretary to the Lord Lieutenant of Ireland and an MP, and helped to establish *The Spectator*.

## Henry Aldrich

If all be true that I do think,
There are five reasons we should drink;
Good wine – a friend – or being dry –
Or lest we should be by and by –
Or any other reason why.

*Reasons for Drinking*

Henry Aldrich (1647–1710) was an English scholar who became dean of Christ Church, Oxford, in 1689 and remained in office until his death. He designed the Peckwater Quadrangle at Christ Church, adapted anthems and church music, and wrote some humorous verse.

## Hans Christian Andersen

Where words fail, music speaks.

*Quoted in Reader's Digest,*
*March 1980*

Hans Christian Andersen (1805–85) was a Danish writer. The son of a shoemaker, he was born at Odense and his first book was published when he was only seventeen but it was not until 1829 that he attracted notice. In 1835 his novel *The Improvisatore* brought him popularity and he began to compose the immortal fairy tales which have since been translated into a great many languages.

## Matthew Arnold

The sea is calm tonight.
The tide is full, the moon lies fair
Upon the Straits.

*Dover Beach*

Runs it not here, the track by Childsworth Farm,
Past the high wood, to where the elm-tree crowns
The hill behind whose ridge the sunset flames?

*Thyrsis*

Once I knew each field, each flower, each stick,
And with the country-folk acquaintance made –

*Thyrsis*

Matthew Arnold (1822–88), the British poet and son of the famous Doctor Arnold, headmaster of Rugby School, was elected professor of poetry at Oxford. He wrote a classical tragedy (*Merope*) and *New Poems*, and these were followed by his *Essays in Criticism*, some studies in education, *Literature and Dogma* and *Culture and Anarchy*.

## Margot Asquith

He has a brilliant mind until he makes it up.

*Of Sir Stafford Cripps*

She tells enough white lies to ice a cake.

*Of a female acquaintance*

I saw him riding in the Row, clinging to his horse like a string of onions.

*Of Lord Hugh Cecil*

Very clever, but his brains go to his head.

*Of F. E. Smith*

She's as tough as an ox. She'll be turned into OXO when she dies.

*Of a friend*

Margot Asquith (1868–1945) was originally Margot Tennant, daughter of Sir Charles Tennant, a rich Glasgow industrialist. In 1894 she married into the famous Asquith family and became known as a celebrated wit, but her volumes of memoirs offended many by their lack of reticence. As wife of the Liberal Prime Minister she had a wide circle of friends and acquaintances.

# Jane Austen

Where an opinion is general, it is usually correct.

It is a truth universally acknowledged, that a single man in possession of a good fortune must be in want of a wife.
*Pride and Prejudice*

One half of the world cannot understand the pleasures of the other.
*Emma*

Jane Austen (1775–1817) was born at Steventon in Hampshire, where her father was rector. She lived an uneventful life, first at her birthplace and later at Bath, Southampton and Chawton. Of her completed novels, *Sense and Sensibility* appeared in 1811, *Pride and Prejudice* in 1813, *Mansfield Park* in 1814, *Emma* in December 1815, and *Northanger Abbey* and *Persuasion* posthumously in 1818.

# Francis Bacon

It is a strange desire men have, to seek power and to lose liberty.

Virtue is like a rich stone, best plain set.

It is as natural to die as to be born; and to a little infant, perhaps, the one is as painful as the other.
*Essays*

God Almighty first planted a garden; and, indeed, it is the purest of human pleasures.
*Essays*

Francis Bacon (1561–1626) was first Baron Verulam and Viscount St Albans, the younger son of Sir Nicholas Bacon, Lord Keeper in Queen Elizabeth's reign. He went through the various steps of the legal profession and entered Parliament in 1584. He wrote papers on public affairs, including a 'Letter of Advice' to Queen Elizabeth urging strong measures against the Catholics, and he became friendly with the Earl of Essex, who treated him with generosity and helped to further his career.

## Hylda Baker

Punctuality is something that if you have it, nobody is ever around to appreciate it.

Hylda Baker (1909–82) was a British comedienne who established herself in northern music-hall tradition and in such films as *Saturday Night and Sunday Morning, Up the Junction* and *Nearest and Dearest*.

## Pierre Balmain

The trick of wearing mink is to look as though you are wearing a cloth coat. The trick of wearing a cloth coat is to look as though you are wearing mink.

*Newspaper report*

Pierre Alexandre Balmain (1914–) was educated at the Lycée de Chambéry and Ecole des Beaux-Arts, Paris. He was a dress designer with Molyneux and then with Lucien Lelong, and became established as a couturier in 1946.

## Honoré de Balzac

Love is perhaps but gratitude for pleasure.

A good husband is never the first to go to sleep at night or the last to awake in the morning.

Children! You bring them into the world, and they drive you out of it.

The man who can govern a woman can govern a nation.

Laws are spider webs that catch little flies, but cannot hold big ones.

Honoré de Balzac (1799–1850) was the son of the director of the City Hospital at Tours. After studying law he turned to literature, but at first with little success. From 1829 onwards he wrote many novels which were to become famous.

# J.M. Barrie

The God to whom little boys say their prayers has a face very like their mother's.

It's a sort of bloom on a woman. If you have it [charm] you don't need to have anything else.

*What Every Woman Knows*

His lordship may compel us to be equal upstairs, but there will never be equality in the servants' hall.

*The Admirable Crichton*

J.M. Barrie (Sir James Matthew Barrie, 1860–1937) was a Scottish novelist and dramatist. He became editorial writer for the *Nottingham Journal* in 1883 but turning to fiction he had great success, particularly with *Peter Pan, Mary Rose* and *Dear Brutus*.

# John Barrymore

The way to fight a woman is with your hat. Grab it and run.

John Barrymore (1882–1942) was a celebrated American stage and screen actor, brother of Ethel and Lionel Barrymore. He was an idol with a great 'profile' and became famous as a romantic movie star of the twenties, but later he squandered his talents in inferior comedies and developed an alcohol problem.

# Max Beerbohm

You cannot make a man by standing a sheep on its legs. But by standing a flock of sheep in that position you can make a crowd of men.

Sir Max Beerbohm (1872–1956) was an English writer who was the half-brother of the actor-manager Sir Herbert Beerbohm-Tree. He contributed to *The Yellow Book of Essays* and succeeded Shaw as dramatic critic to the *Saturday Review*. He was knighted in 1939.

## Brendan Behan

We have flower battles just as they do in Nice. Only here we throw the pots as well.

*On the Dublin Festival, 10 July 1960*

Brendan Behan (1923 – 64), Irish author and playwright, was a housepainter by trade. He started writing in 1951, achieving success in 1956 with his play *The Quare Fellow* which was based on his own prison experiences. Other works followed, including *Borstal Boy*, *The Hostage* and *Brendan Behan's Island*.

## Hilaire Belloc

How did the party go in Portland Square?
I cannot tell you: Juliet was not there.
And how did Lady Gaster's party go?
Juliet was next to me, and I do not know.

*Blinding Love*

I'm tired of Love: I'm still more tired of Rhyme.
But Money gives me pleasure all the time.

*Epigrams*

The Llama is a woolly sort of fleecy hairy goat,
With an indolent expression and an undulating throat.

*More Beasts for Worse Children*

I will hold my house in the high wood
Within a walk of the sea,
And the men that were boys when I was a boy
Shall sit and drink with me.

*The South Country*

Joseph Hilaire Pierre Belloc (1870 – 1953) was the son of a French barrister and an English mother. He founded the *Eye-Witness* in collaboration with Cecil Chesterton, with whom he also wrote a political work entitled *The Party System*. He also worked with G.K. Chesterton, and his literary versatility is shown by his nonsense verse, his historical studies of Danton, Robespierre and James II, his *History of England*, and various satires.

## Robert Benchley

I do most of my work sitting down; that's where I shine.

Robert Benchley (1889–1945), the American humorist, was born at Worcester, Mass, went to New York as a journalist and became drama editor of the *New Yorker*. His books *Of All Things* and *Benchley Beside Himself* demonstrate his fine ability to extract humour from daily life.

## Edmund Clerihew Bentley

Sir Christopher Wren
Said, 'I am going to dine with some men.
If anyone calls
Tell them I'm designing St. Paul's.'

The art of Biography
Is different from Geography.
Geography is about maps,
But Biography is about chaps.

What I like about Clive
Is that he is no longer alive.
There is a great deal to be said
For being dead.

Edmund Clerihew Bentley (1876–1956) was the author of *Trent's Last Case*, a famous detective story. He invented the 'clerihew', an epigrammatic verse-form consisting of two rhymed couplets, usually dealing with the character or career of a well-known person.

## Irving Berlin

We depend largely on tricks, we writers of songs. There is no such thing as a new melody.

Irving Berlin (1888–), an American composer of popular songs, wrote such hits as *Alexander's Ragtime Band*, *Always* and *Annie Get your Gun*. Born in Russia and named Israel Baline, he settled in America in 1893 and used Irving Berlin as a pseudonym.

13

## Josh Billings

It is the little bits of things that fret and worry us; we can dodge an elephant, but we can't dodge a fly.

Consider the postage stamp; its usefulness consists in the ability to stick to one thing till it gets there.

There is one kind of laugh that I always recommend; it looks out of the eye first with a merry twinkle, then it creeps down on to its hands and knees and plays around the mouth like a pretty moth around the haze of a candle.

There are two things in this life for which we are never fully prepared: twins.

Thrice is he armed that hath his quarrel just
But four times he who gets his blow in fust.
*Josh Billings, His Sayings*

Josh Billings (1818–85) was the pseudonym of Henry Wheeler Shaw, an American humorous writer. His popular work *Josh Billings, His Sayings* depended for its humour on mis-spellings, puns and malapropisms.

## Laurence Binyon

They shall not grow old, as we that are left grow old;
Age shall not weary them, nor the years condemn.
At the going down of the sun, and in the morning,
We will remember them.
*For the Fallen*

Laurence Binyon (1869–1943) was born at Lancaster, the son of a clergyman, and became Keeper of prints and drawings at the British Museum. He published some studies of English and Eastern art, but is best remembered for his fine ode *For the Fallen*, which was written in 1914.

## William Blake

Tyger! Tyger! burning bright
In the forests of the night,
What immortal hand or eye
Could frame thy fearful symmetry?

*Songs of Experience: The Tyger*

Bring me my bow of burning gold!
Bring me my arrows of desire!
Bring me my spear! O clouds, unfold!
Bring me my chariot of fire.

I will not cease from mental fight,
Nor shall my sword sleep in my hand,
Till we have built Jerusalem
In England's green and pleasant land.

*Milton, Preface*

To see a World in a Grain of Sand,
And a Heaven in a Wild Flower –
Hold Infinity in the palm of your hand,
And Eternity in an hour.

*Auguries of Innocence*

William Blake (1757–1827) was apprenticed to an engraver and studied at the Academy under Reynolds. He engraved the illustrations for his *Book of Thel, Marriage of Heaven and Hell* and *Song of Los*, but after the failure of an exhibition in 1809 he retired from engraving. His works include *Milton, Jerusalem* and the fragmentary *Everlasting Gospel*.

## James Boswell

I never shall forget the indulgence with which he (Samuel Johnson) treated Hodge, his cat, for whom he himself used to go out and buy oysters, lest the servant having that trouble should take a dislike to the poor creature.

*The Life of Samuel Johnson, Hodge the Cat*

While the Dictionary was going forward, Johnson lived part of the time in Holborn, part in Gough Square, Fleet Street, and he had an upper room fitted up like a counting-house for the purpose in which he gave to the copyists their several tasks.

15

The words, partly taken from other dictionaries, and partly supplied by himself, having been first written down with spaces left between them, he delivered in writing their etymologies, definitions, and various significations.

The authorities were copied from the books themselves, in which he had marked the passages with a black-lead pencil, the traces of which could easily be effected.

I have seen several of them, in which that trouble had not been taken, so that they were just as when used by the copyists.

*The Life of Samuel Johnson*

James Boswell (1740–95) was a Scottish biographer and man of letters. He studied law but centred his ambition on literature and politics. He is most famous for his biography, *The Life of Samuel Johnson*. Their first meeting was in 1763, and this was followed in 1764 with the formation of the Literary Club, the original members of which included Reynolds, Burke and Goldsmith. Garrick and C.J. Fox joined soon after, and it was here that Boswell became so closely associated with Johnson and took great interest in the formation of his *Dictionary* (published in 1755).

## Bessie Braddock

Right now the basic insecurity the workers feel is this; they are haunted by the spectre of the van driving up to the door to take away the TV set.

*19.6.1955*

Bessie (Elizabeth Margaret) Braddock JP (1899–1970) was Labour MP for the Exchange Division of Liverpool from 1945 onwards. She was the daughter of Mary Bamber JP and Hugh Bamber, and married John Braddock in 1922. For a time she was President of Liverpool Trades and Labour Council.

16

## Rupert Brooke

If I should die, think only this of me:
That there's some corner of a foreign field
That is for ever England.

*The Soldier*

Stands the Church clock at ten to three?
And is there honey still for tea?

*The Old Vicarage:*
*Grantchester*

God! I will pack, and take a train,
And get me to England once again!
For England's the one land, I know,
Where men with splendid hearts may go;
And Cambridgeshire, of all England,
The shire for men who understand;
And of *that* district I prefer
The lovely hamlet, Grantchester.

*The Old Vicarage:*
*Grantchester*

Rupert Chawner Brooke (1887–1915) was the son of a
master at Rugby, where he was educated before going to
King's College, Cambridge. His first volume of verse was
published in 1911, and in the years 1913–1914 he
travelled in America and the South Seas. With the
outbreak of war in 1914 he took part in the unsuccessful
defence of Antwerp, and early in 1915 he was sent to the
Mediterranean, where he died at Scyros. A memorial to
him has been erected there.

## Elizabeth Barrett Browning

But the child's sob in the silence curses deeper
Than the strong man in his wrath.

*The Cry of the Children*

'Yes,' I answered you last night:
'No,' this morning, sir, I say.
Colours seen by candle-light
Will not look the same by day.

*The Lady's Yes*

WST-B

Unless you can muse in a crowd all day
On the absent face that fixed you:
Unless you can love, as the angels may,
With the breadth of Heaven betwixt you:
Unless you can dream that his faith is fast,
Through behoving and unbehoving;
Unless you can die when the dream is past –
Oh, never call it loving:-

*A Woman's Shortcomings*

Elizabeth Barrett Browning (1806 – 61) was the daughter of wealthy Edward Moulton Barrett. In youth she lived chiefly in Herefordshire, but eventually the family moved to Wimpole Street, London. Elizabeth began to write poetry when she was quite young, and when a riding accident barred her for some years from an active life she gave her whole time to reading and writing. In 1844 she published *Verses*, a volume including *The Cry of the Children*, which made her name known. Because of her poetry Robert Browning visited her and fell in love with her.

## Robert Browning

The year's at the spring,
And day's at the morn;
Morning's at seven;
The hill-side's dew-pearled;
The lark's on the wing;
The snail's on the thorn;
God's in his heaven –
All's right with the world!

*Pippa Passes: Morning*

You'll love me yet: – and I can tarry
Your love's protracted growing:
June reared that bunch of flowers you carry,
From seeds of April's sowing.

*Pippa Passes: Evening*

That's the wise thrush; he sings each song twice over,
Lest you should think he never could recapture
The first fine careless rapture!

*Home-thoughts, from Abroad*

18

Oh, to be in England
Now that April's there...

*Home-thoughts, from Abroad*

There may be Heaven; there must be hell;
Meantime, there is our earth here – well!

*Time's Revenges*

Hamelin Town's in Brunswick,
By famous Hanover city;
The river Weser, deep and wide,
Washes its walls on the southern side.

*The Pied Piper of Hamelin*

Into the street the Piper stept,
Smiling first a little smile,
As if he knew what magic slept
In his quiet pipe the while...

*The Pied Piper of Hamelin*

And the mutterings grew to a grumbling,
And the grumbling grew to a mighty rumbling;
And out of the houses the rats came tumbling...

*The Pied Piper of Hamelin*

From street to street he piped, advancing,
And step by step they followed, dancing.

*The Pied Piper of Hamelin*

Robert Browning (1812–89), born at Camberwell, was
the son of a clerk in the Bank of England. Educated at a
private school and at home, he travelled a great deal in
Europe. Devoting his whole life to poetry, he published
his first piece *Pauline* in 1833, but in 1835 his *Paracelsus*
attracted the friendly notice of Carlyle, Wordsworth and
other men of letters. He married Elizabeth Barrett and
lived with her in Italy, but when she died he returned to
London and published many more pieces of poetry.

## George Burns

My secret for longevity? Drinking martinis, smoking
cigars.

19

George Burns (1898–) first made his name in Vaudeville as a dancer. Then he teamed up with Gracie Allen, and together they toured the USA and Europe, making their radio debut with the BBC. In 1976 he received an Academy Award for Best Supporting Actor in the film *The Sunshine Boys*.

## Robert Burns

Wee, sleekit, cow'rin', tim'rous beastie,
O, what a panic's in thy breastie!

*To a Mouse*

From scenes like these old Scotia's grandeur springs,
That make her loved at home, revered abroad:
Princes and lords are but the breath of kings,
'An honest man's the noblest work of God'.

*The Cotter's Saturday Night*

Whare sits our sulky sullen dame,
Gathering her brows like gathering storm,
Nursing her wrath to keep it warm.

*Tam o'Shanter*

Robert Burns (1759–96) was the son of a cotter and was educated by his father. From 1784 to 1788 he farmed, but during that period he wrote some of his best work – *The Cotter's Saturday Night*, *The Twa Dogs*, *Halloween*, *The Jolly Beggars*, *To a Mouse* and *To a Mountain Daisy*. In 1786 he published the Kilmarnock edition of his early poems, which made him famous. A second edition of his poems brought him £500, which enabled him to settle down on a small farm and marry one of his many loves, Jean Armour. About the same time he received an exciseman's appointment, and this became his principal means of support. He then wrote *Tam o'Shanter* and *Captain Matthew Henderson*, but little else of importance.

## Samuel Butler

Brigands demand your money or your life; women require both.

Samuel Butler (1612–80), the English satirical poet, was for a time page to the Countess of Kent, and later became steward of Ludlow Castle. He was the author of *Hudi bras*, a much-quoted mock-heroic poem satirising the hypocrisy, churlishness, greed, pride and casuistry of the Presbyterians and Independents.

## George Gordon Noel Byron

'Tis pleasant, sure, to see one's name in print;
A book's a book, although there's nothing in't.
*English Bards and Scotch Reviewers*

I assure you there are things in Derbyshire as noble as in Greece or Switzerland.

Seek roses in December – ice in June;
Hope constancy in wind, or corn in chaff;
Believe a woman or an epitaph,
Or any other thing that's false, before
You trust in critics, who themselves are sore.
*English Bards and Scotch Reviewers*

Maidens, like moths, are ever caught by glare.
*Childe Harold's Pilgrimage*

George Gordon Noel Byron (1788–1824), sixth baron, the son of Captain John Byron, was born in London and came into the title when he was ten years old. He was educated at Harrow and Trinity College, Cambridge, and while at Cambridge he printed his *Hours of Idleness* which was first called *Juvenilia* and published in 1807. For several years he travelled abroad, visiting Portugal, Spain, Greece and the Levant, and on his return he published the first two cantos of *Childe Harold*.

## Thomas Carlyle

The block of granite which was an obstacle in the pathway of the weak, became a stepping-stone in the pathway of the strong.

The three great elements of modern civilization, Gunpowder, Printing, and the Protestant Religion.
*Critical and Miscellaneous Essays*

Happy the people whose annals are blank in history books!

*Frederick the Great, Bk XVI*

No great man lives in vain. The history of the world is but the biography of great men.

*Heroes and Hero Worship*

Thomas Carlyle (1795–1881) was a Scottish author who studied for the Presbyterian ministry but later gave up the Church and combined study of the law with miscellaneous literary work. He established his reputation with *The French Revolution*, which is said to be still unrivalled in its vividness of narration.

## Hoagy Carmichael

The trouble with doing nothing is that you can never take any time off.

Hoagy Carmichael (1899–1982) was an American song composer and lyricist, best known for his *Stardust* and *In the Cool, Cool, Cool of the Evening*. He was also a slow-speaking actor of light supporting roles, usually involving his singing at the piano. He wrote two autobiographies, *The Stardust Road* and *Sometimes I Wonder*.

## Lewis Carroll

'You are old, Father William,' the young man said,
'And your hair has become very white;
And yet you incessantly stand on your head –
Do you think, at your age, it is right?'

'In my youth,' Father William replied to his son,
'I feared it might injure the brain;
But now that I'm perfectly sure I have none,
Why, I do it again and again.'

*Alice's Adventures in
Wonderland*

The Queen was in a furious passion, and went stamping about, and shouting 'Off with his head!' or 'Off with her head!' about once in a minute.

*Alice's Adventures in
Wonderland*

'What is the use of a book', thought Alice, 'without pictures or conversations?'

*Alice's Adventures in Wonderland*

Take care of the sense, and the sounds will take care of themselves.

*Alice's Adventures in Wonderland*

'Reeling and Writhing, of course, to begin with,' the Mock Turtle replied; 'and then the different branches of Arithmetic – Ambition, Distraction, Uglification, and Derision.'

*Alice's Adventures in Wonderland*

Curtsey while you're thinking what to say. It saves time.

*Through the Looking-Glass*

The rule is, jam to-morrow and jam yesterday – but never jam to-day.

*Through the Looking-Glass*

You see, it's like a portmanteau – there are two meanings packed up into one word.

*Through the Looking-Glass*

'Twas brillig and the slithy toves
Did gyre and gimble in the wabe.
All mincing were the borogoves
And the nome raths outgrabe.

*Through the Looking-Glass: Jabberwocky*

He would answer to 'Hi!' or to any loud cry,
Such as 'Fry me!' or 'Fritter my wig!'
To 'What-you-may-call-um!' or 'What-was-his-name!'
But especially 'Thing-um-a-jig!'

*The Hunting of the Snark*

Lewis Carroll (1839–98) was the pseudonym of Charles Lutwidge Dodgson, a mathematician and writer of children's books. He became a lecturer in mathematics at Oxford and published books on the subject, but became famous for *Alice's Adventures in Wonderland*. This grew out of a story told by Dodgson to amuse three little girls, including the original Alice – Alice Liddell, daughter of the dean of Christ Church. Later he published *Through the Looking Glass* and *The Hunting of the Snark*.

## Jimmy Carter

I am convinced that UFO's exist, because I have seen one.

*16.6.1976*

I'm tired of our taxing the poor people in our rich country and sending the money to rich people in poor countries.

*On taxes, 29.8.1976*

Jimmy Carter (James Earl Carter Jnr; 1924 –), American farmer and politician, was educated at Plains High School, Georgia, Southwestern College, Georgia Institute of Technology, and US Naval Academy, Annapolis. He served in the US Navy from 1946 to 1953 and attained the rank of Lieut-Commander. He became a peanut farmer and warehouseman in 1953, in the business of Carter Farms, Georgia; State Senator of Georgia from 1962 to 1966; Governor of Georgia from 1971 to 1974; and President of the United States of America in January 1977.

## Barbara Cartland

I'll wager you that in ten years it will be fashionable again to be a virgin.

*20.6.1976*

There's no substitute for moonlight and kissing.

*11.9.1977*

Barbara Cartland (1901–) is a very popular writer. She published her first novel at the age of twenty-one, which ran into five editions. Since then she has written hundreds of romantic novels as well as biographies, cookery books, plays, and some verse, and has designed and organised many pageants in aid of charity. She has also made frequent radio and television appearances.

## Enrico Caruso

The requisite of a singer – a big chest, a big mouth, ninety per cent memory, ten per cent intelligence, lots of hard work, and something in the heart.

Enrico Caruso (1873–1921) was an Italian operatic tenor. Born in Naples, he made his first appearance on the stage there at twenty-one, and later achieved great success in Milan in Puccini's *La Bohème*. Subsequently he won world-wide fame and appeared in many European and American cities.

## Edith Cavell

I realise that patriotism is not enough. I must have no hatred or bitterness towards anyone.
*Last words, 12.10.1915*

Edith Louisa Cavell (1865–1915) was born in Norfolk. She was trained at the London Hospital and became matron of a medical institute in Brussels. During the German occupation she harboured wounded and refugee soldiers and aided their escape into Holland. Denounced by a renegade, she was tried by Court Martial and shot.

## Miguel de Cervantes

Don't put too fine a point to your wit for fear it should get blunted.

We cannot all be friars, and many are the ways by which God leads His children home.

The best sauce in the world is hunger.
*Don Quixote*

There are but two families in the world, as my grand-mother used to say, the Haves and the Havenots.
*Don Quixote*

Blessings on him who invented sleep, the mantle that covers all human thoughts.
*Don Quixote*

Miguel de Cervantes (1547–1616) was a Spanish novelist and dramatist. Born at Alcala, the son of an apothecary, he lived for a time in Madrid and then went to Italy. In 1570 he became a soldier, but was taken prisoner by the Barbary pirates and spent five years as a prisoner at Algiers. Cervantes wrote a great deal of verse, a number of dramas, and the *Exemplary Novels* which give a good idea of the life of the time, but he is known best of all by his immortal novel *Don Quixote* which was published in two parts.

## Nicholas Chamfort

A day is wasted without laughter.

The highest qualities often unfit a man for society. We don't take ingots with us to market, we take silver or small change.

Society is composed of two large classes; those who have more dinners than appetites, and those who have more appetite than dinners.

In great matters men try to show themselves to their best advantage; in small matters they show themselves as they are.

Sebastien Roch Nicholas Chamfort (1741–94) was a French writer and wit. At the outbreak of the Revolution he joined the Jacobins, took part in the storming of the Bastille, and bitterly attacked the National Convention. He mortally wounded himself when about to be arrested. He is best known for his *Maximes*, which was published posthumously, but he was also author of comedies, literary criticisms, letters and verse.

## G.K. Chesterton

The home is not the one tame place in the world of adventure. It is the one wild place in the world of rules and set tasks.

There are no rules of architecture for a castle in the clouds.

A yawn is a silent shout.

Old Noah he had an ostrich farm, and fowls on the largest scale...
He ate his egg with a ladle in an egg-cup big as a pail.
And the soup he took was Elephant Soup, and the fish he took was whale.
But they all were small to the cellar he took when he set out to sail.

*Wine, Water and Song*

Gilbert Keith Chesterton (1874 – 1936) was a British author, born in London. He studied art, but quickly turned to journalism. In poetry his best work was in satire, particularly in his *Wine, Water and Song* and *The Ballad of the White Horse*. His most famous novels are those dealing with the adventures of the naïve priest-detective, Father Brown.

## Sir Winston Churchill

I have always been surprised to see some of our Bishops and clergy making such heavy weather about reconciling the Bible story with modern scientific and historical knowledge. Why do they want to reconcile them?

If you are the recipient of a message which cheers your heart and fortifies your soul, which promises you reunion with those you have loved in a world of larger opportunity and wider sympathies, why should you worry about the shape or colour of the travel-stained envelope; whether it is duly stamped, whether the date on the postmark is right or wrong?

These matters may be puzzling, but they are certainly not important. What is important is the message and the benefits to you of receiving it.

*My Early Life*

I have nothing to offer but blood, toil, tears and sweat.
*Speech in House of Commons, 13.5.1940*

We shall not flag or fail. We shall fight in France, we shall fight on the seas and the oceans, we shall fight with growing confidence and growing strength in the air, we shall defend our island, whatever the cost may be...
*Speech in House of Commons, 4.6.1940*

Let us therefore brace ourselves to our duty and so bear ourselves that if the British Empire and its Commonwealth last for a thousand years men will still say, 'This was their finest hour'.

*Speech in House of Commons, 18.6.1940*

The gratitude of every home in our island, in our Empire, and indeed throughout the world, except in the abodes of the guilty, goes out to the British airmen who, undaunted by odds, unwearied in their constant challenge and mortal danger, are turning the tide of the world war by their prowess and by their devotion. Never in the field of human conflict was so much owed by so many to so few.

*Speech in House of Commons, 20.8.1940*

These two great organisations of the English-speaking democracies, the British Empire and the United States, will have to be somewhat mixed up together in some of their affairs ... I do not view the process with any misgivings. I could not stop it if I wished; no one can stop it. Like the Mississippi, it just keeps rolling along. Let it roll. Let it roll on full flood, inexorable, irresistible, benignant, to broader lands and better days.

*Speech in House of Commons, 20.8.1940*

Give us the tools, and we will finish the job.

*Broadcast address, 9.2.1941*

It becomes still more difficult to reconcile Japanese action with prudence or even with sanity. What kind of people do they think we are?

*Speech to US Congress after Pearl Harbour, 26.12.1941*

When I warned them [the French Government] that Britain would fight on alone whatever they did their generals told their Prime Minister and his divided Cabinet, 'In three weeks England will have had her neck wrung like a chicken.' Some chicken! some neck!

*Speech to Canadian Senate and House of Commons, 30.12.1941*

Sir Winston Leonard Spencer Churchill (1874 – 1965) was a descendant of the great Duke of Marlborough. Churchill was born at Blenheim Palace, the elder son of
28

Lord Randolph Churchill and his American wife, Jenny Jerome. In 1895 he was commissioned in the 4th Hussars and saw active service in a series of minor campaigns. During the Boer War he was the war correspondent of the *Morning Post*, was taken prisoner, then made a dramatic escape from imprisonment in Pretoria.

In 1900 Churchill was elected Conservative MP for Oldham – but he disagreed with Chamberlain's tariff reform policy and joined the Liberals. Later he became President of the Board of Trade, and introduced legislation for the establishment of Labour Exchanges. In 1910 he became Home Secretary and was present at the siege of Sidney Street.

As First Lord of the Admiralty he became involved in controversy over the Dardanelles operation, and in 1916 was in the trenches of France with the Royal Scots Fusiliers. As Minister of Munitions under Lloyd George, he had much to do with the development of the tank. During the Second World War he was a great war leader, famous for his rallying speeches.

Churchill was also a distinguished writer. He won the Nobel Prize for Literature in 1953.


## John Clare

If life had a second edition, how I would correct the proofs.

*Letter to a friend*

John Clare (1793–1864), the poet, was born near Peterborough, the son of a farm labourer, and passed most of his days in poverty, in spite of an annuity from the Duke of Exeter. He wrote *Poems Descriptive of Rural Life, The Village Minstrel* and *The Shepherd's Calendar*.


## Arthur Hugh Clough

Do not adultery commit;
Advantage rarely comes of it.

*The Latest Decalogue*

Grace is given of God, but knowledge is bought in the market.

*The Bothie of
Tober-na-Vuolich*

When daylight comes, comes in the light,
In front the sun climbs slow, how slowly,
But westward, look, the land is bright.

*Say not the Struggle Naught*
*Availeth*

Arthur Hugh Clough (1819–61), the British poet, was
born in Liverpool, the son of a rich cotton merchant, and
was at Rugby under the famous Doctor Arnold. His
poem *Say not the Struggle Naught Availeth* was made
famous during the Second World War because it was
quoted by Sir Winston Churchill in one of his war
speeches.

## S. T. Coleridge

Therefore all seasons shall be sweet to thee,
Whether the summer clothe the general earth
With greenness, or redbreast sit and sing
Betwixt the tufts of snow on the bare branch.

*All Seasons Shall be Sweet*

They stood aloof, the scars remaining,
Like cliffs which had been rent asunder...

*Christabel*

The Knight's bones are dust,
And his good sword rust –
His soul is with the saints, I trust.

*The Knight's Tomb*

Not the poem which we have *read*, but that to which we
*return* with the greatest pleasure, possesses the genuine
power, and claims the name of *essential poetry*.

*Biographia Literaria*

I wish our clever young poets would remember my
homely definitions of prose and poetry; that is, prose =
words in their best order; – poetry = the *best* words in
the best order.

*Table Talk*

Samuel Taylor Coleridge (1772–1834), son of the vicar of
Ottery St Mary, Devon, was educated at Christ's Hospital and Jesus College, Cambridge. He contributed verses

to the *Morning Chronicle* and collaborated with Words-worth in *Lyrical Ballads*, which contained his *Ancient Mariner*. In 1798 he visited Germany, where he became interested in German literature and philosophy. The best of his criticism is found in *Biographia Literaria* and *Table Talk*.

## Confucius

If husband sent too often to doghouse, he go at last to cathouse.

Confucius (c550 – 478BC) is a Latinised form of K'ung Fu-tzu (K'ung the master) and this Chinese sage was born in Lu, a small state in what later became the province of Shangtun. His early years were spent in poverty, but at fifteen his mind was set on learning. Gradually he attracted a number of disciples to his system of cosmology, politics and ethics. He revised the ancient Chinese scriptures, and on his death was buried with great pomp.

## William Congreve

Music hath charms to soothe a savage breast,
To soften rocks, or bend a knotted oak.
*The Mourning Bride*

Heav'n has no rage, like love to hatred turn'd,
Nor Hell a fury like a woman scorn'd.
*The Mourning Bride*

Let us be very strange and well-bred: Let us be as strange as if we had been married a great while, and as well-bred as if we were not married at all.
*The Way of the World*

Defer not till to-morrow to be wise.
To-morrow's sun to thee may never rise.
*Letter to Viscount Cobham*

William Congreve (1670 – 1729) was born near Leeds, was a friend of Swift at Trinity College, Dublin, and then studied law in London. He won immediate success with his first comedy *The Old Bachelor* and this was followed by *The Double Dealer*, *Love for Love* and his tragedy *The*

*Mourning Bride*. His masterpiece *The Way of the World* was at first regarded as a failure. Congreve is regarded by many people as the most brilliant of the Restoration comic dramatists.

## Joseph Conrad

Women's rougher, simpler, more upright judgment embraces the whole truth, which their tact, their mistrust of masculine idealism, ever prevents them from speaking in its entirety.

*Chance*

Joseph Conrad (Teodor Josef Konrad Korzeniowski; 1854–1924) was born of Polish parents in the Ukraine, and accompanied them when they were exiled to northern Russia. For a time he went to school in Cracow, but in 1874 he became a member of the crew of a French vessel, which satisfied a long-felt craving for a seafaring life. In 1884 he was naturalised as a British subject. In 1894 he left the sea and devoted himself to literature.

## William Cowper

Now stir the fire, and close the shutters fast,
Let fall the curtains, wheel the sofa round.

*The Task – Winter Evening*

To-morrow is our wedding-day,
And then we will repair
Unto the Bell at Edmonton
All in a chaise and pair.

*John Gilpin*

O'erjoy'd was he to find
That, though on pleasure she was bent,
She had a frugal mind.

*John Gilpin*

How much a dunce that has been sent to roam
Excels a dunce that has been kept at home.

*The Progress of Error*

Pernicious weed! whose scent the fair annoys,
Unfriendly to society's chief joys,
Thy worst effect is banishing for hours
The sex whose presence civilizes ours.

*Conversation*

Twelve years have elapsed since I last took a view
Of my favourite field, and the bank where they [poplars]
grew;
And now in the grass behold they are laid,
And the tree is my seat that once lent me a shade.

*The Poplar-Field*

William Cowper (1731–1800) began his literary work
with the hymns he wrote with the Reverend John
Newton, but later Mrs Unwin persuaded him to write
poetry, and a volume of poems appeared in 1782. Lady
Austen told him the story of John Gilpin, which became
the subject of one of his most popular poems, and she
also persuaded him to write his greatest work *The Task*.

## Oliver Cromwell

What shall we do with this bauble? There, take it away.

*Of the Mace, when dismissing*
*Parliament, 20.4.1653*

Mr. Lely, I desire you would use all your skill to paint
my picture truly like me, and not flatter me at all; but
remark all these roughnesses, pimples, warts, and everything as you see me, otherwise I will never pay a farthing
for it.

*Remark: Walpole's Anecdotes*
*of Painting*

Oliver Cromwell (1599–1658) was born at Huntingdon,
the son of a small landowner, and was educated at the
local grammar school and at Cambridge. Active in the
events leading to the Civil War, he raised a troop of horse
and was engaged in the Battle of Edgehill. After that he
raised more cavalry forces, which were chiefly responsible for the victory at Marston Moor. Cromwell was a
member of the special commission which tried the King
and condemned him to death, and later he assumed the
title of Protector, with almost royal powers.

## Bette Davis

Morality to me is honesty, integrity, character. Old-
fashioned words. There are new words now that excuse
everything.

Give me the days of heroes and villains. The people you can bravo or hiss. There was a truth to them that all the slick credulity of today cannot touch.

How wonderful it would be to know again where we stand and which side we're on.

*The Lonely Life*

Bette Davis (1908–), the American actress and film star, was born Ruth Elizabeth Davis in Massachusetts. She entered films in 1930 and established her reputation with *Of Human Bondage*. Later films included *Dangerous* and *Jezebel*, both of which earned her Academy Awards. Her career has been an outstanding one and she has written two autobiographies, *The Lonely Life* (1962) and *Mother Goddam* (1975).

## W.H. Davies

What is this life if, full of care,
We have no time to stand and stare?
No time to stand beneath the boughs
And stare as long as sheep or cows.

*Leisure*

Welcome to you, rich Autumn days,
Here comes the cold, leaf-picking wind,
When golden stocks are seen in fields –
All standing arm-in-arm entwined.

*Rich Days*

William Henry Davies (1871–1940), the British poet, went to America and for years lived the life of a hobo. He lost his right foot while 'riding the rods', and later returned to England and published his first volume of poems *Soul's Destroyer*. While living the life of a wandering pedlar he published more volumes of simple verse and the prose work *The Autobiography of a Supertramp*.

## Sammy Davis Junior

I invented controversy, but not on purpose.

My own rules are very simple. Don't hurt nobody. Be nice to people.

Sammy Davis Junior (1925–) began his theatrical life by taking part in films, then made Vaudeville appearances with a trio. He became singer, dancer, impressionist and recorder of songs for various companies, and has written his autobiography, which he has called *Yes I Can*.

## Daniel Defoe

He bade me observe it, and I should always find, that the calamities of life were shared among the upper and the lower part of mankind; but that the middle station had the fewest disasters.

*Robinson Crusoe*

Wherever God erects a house of prayer,
The Devil always builds a chapel there;
And 'twill be found upon examination,
The latter has the largest congregation.

*The True-born Englishman*

Daniel Defore (1660 – 1731) was born in London, the son of James Foe, a butcher, but later he changed his name by adding the prefix. Daniel took part in Monmouth's rebellion, then joined William III's army in 1688. In 1701 he published *The True-born Englishman*, a satirical poem about the popular prejudice against a king of foreign birth, and in 1702 a notorious pamphlet entitled *The Shortest Way with the Dissenters*. For this he was fined, imprisoned and pilloried. This harsh treatment had a bad effect on him and from then on he became shifty and mercenary in public affairs. The last volume of *Robinson Crusoe* was published in 1719, and in all Defoe published a total of 250 works.

## Charles Dickens

Annual income twenty pounds, annual expenditure nineteen nineteen six, result happiness. Annual income twenty pounds, annual expenditure twenty pounds ought and six, result misery.

*David Copperfield, Mr Micawber*

Father is rather vulgar, my dear. The word Papa, besides, gives a pretty form to the lips. Papa, potatoes, poultry, prunes and prism, are all very good words for the lips; especially prunes and prism.

*Little Dorrit, Mrs General*

Train up a fig-tree in the way it should go, and when you are old sit under the shade of it.

*Dombey and Son, Captain Cuttle*

O let us love our occupations,
Bless the squire and his relations,
Live upon our daily rations,
And always know our proper stations.

*A Christmas Book for Children, The Chimes*

Youth are boarded, clothed, booked, furnished with pocket-money, provided with all necessaries, instructed in all languages living and dead, mathematics, orthography, geometry, astronomy, trigonometry, the use of the globes, algebra, single stick (if required), writing, arithmetic, fortification, and every other branch of classical literature. Terms, twenty guineas per annum. No extras, no vacations, and diet unparalleled.

*Nicholas Nickleby, Mr Squeers's Academy*

C-l-e-a-n, clean, verb active, to make bright, to scour. W-i-n, win, d-e-r, der, winder, or casement. When the boy knows this out of the book, he goes and does it.

*Nicholas Nickleby, Mr Squeers*

With affection beaming in one eye, and calculation shining out of the other.

*Martin Chuzzlewit, Mrs Todgers*

Mr. Weller's knowledge of London was extensive and peculiar.

*Pickwick Papers*

Kent, sir – everybody knows Kent – apples, cherries, hops, and women.

*Pickwick Papers, Jingle*

Miss Bolo rose from the table considerably agitated, and went straight home, in a flood of tears and a sedan chair.

*Pickwick Papers*

It's over, and can't be helped, and that's one consolation as they always say in Turkey, ven they cuts the wrong man's head off.

*Pickwick Papers, Sam Weller*

Accidents will occur in the best-regulated families.
*David Copperfield, Mr Micawber*

Any man may be in good spirits and good temper when he's well dressed.
*Martin Chuzzlewit, Mark Tapley*

'It is', says Chadband, 'the ray of rays, the sun of suns, the moon of moons, the star of stars.'
*Bleak House*

It is a far, far better thing that I do, than I have ever done; it is a far, far better rest I go to, than I have ever known.
*A Tale of Two Cities, Sidney Carton*

I think ... that it is the best club in London.
*Our Mutual Friend, Mr Twemlow on the House of Commons*

Charles Dickens (1812–70), the son of a government clerk who was imprisoned in the Marshalsea prison for debt, used many of his own unhappy experiences in the books he wrote. He received little systematic education although a short period spent working in a blacking factory was followed by three years in a private school. He became a lawyer's clerk, then a reporter in Doctors' Commons, and eventually parliamentary reporter for the *Morning Chronicle*, to which he contributed his *Sketches by Boz*. His *Pickwick Papers* were originally intended as an accompaniment to a series of sporting illustrations, but the adventures of Pickwick outgrew their setting and established Dickens' position as a writer.

## Marlene Dietrich

The average man is more interested in a woman who is interested in him than he is in a woman – any woman – with beautiful legs.

Marlene Dietrich (1901–) was born in Berlin as Maria Magdalena von Losch. A German singer-actress living in America for many years, she became a legend of glamour in films, being known particularly for her part in *The Blue Angel*.

37

## Benjamin Disraeli

Though I sit down now, the time will come when you will hear me.

*Maiden Speech, 7.12.1837*

The right hon. Gentleman [Sir Robert Peel] caught the Whigs bathing, and walked away with their clothes.

*Speech in House of Commons, 28.2.1845*

The question is this: is man an ape or an angel? Now I am on the side of the angels.

*Speech, Oxford 25.11.1864*

A University should be a place of light, of liberty, and of learning.

*Speech in House of Commons, 11.3.1873*

No, it is better not. She would only ask me to take a message to Albert.

*Reply when it was suggested to him as he lay dying that he might like a visit from Queen Victoria*

Every woman should marry – and no man.

*Lothair*

Benjamin Disraeli (1804 – 81), first Earl of Beaconsfield, was the eldest son of Isaac D'Israeli and received his literary training chiefly in his father's library instead of at University. He published his first novel *Vivian Grey* in his twenty-second year. Though hampered by debt, he made the popular grand tour, and published *The Young Duke* in 1831. In 1837 he entered Parliament as Member for Maidstone, and in a few years became the leader of a small group called The Young England Party, whose ideas are described in his novels *Coningsby* and *Tancredi*. In his last year as prime minister, 1880, he published his last novel *Endymion*.

## Dorothy Dix

Drying a widow's tears is one of the most dangerous occupations known to man.

Dorothy Dix (Dorothy Knight Waddy, 1909–70) was the second daughter of William Knight Dix. Educated at St Christopher's School, Hampstead, Lausanne University and University College London, she became a QC in 1957 and a County Court Judge in 1968. She acted as Deputy-Recorder of Deal in 1946, during the absence of Mr Christmas Humphries at the Tokyo War trials.

## Henry Austin Dobson

The ladies of St. James's!
They're painted to the eyes,
Their white it stays for ever,
Their red it never dies.

*The Ladies of St. James's*

But Phyllida, my Phyllida!
Her colour comes, and goes;
It trembles to a lily, –
It wavers to a rose.

*The Ladies of St. James's*

Henry Austin Dobson (1840–1921) was an accomplished writer of light verse, and some of his best work appeared in *Vignettes in Rhyme*, *Proverbs in Porcelain* and *Old World Idylls*.

## Feodor Mikhailovitch Dostoievsky

Man is a pliable animal, a being who gets accustomed to everything.

*The House of the Dead*

Feodor Mikhailovitch Dostoievsky (1821–81) was born in Moscow and educated as an engineer, but soon he began to write. His first book *Poor Folk* was published in 1846, but his political activities led to his arrest and he was sent to Siberia, where he remained for four years. The next three were spent in the army, and after that he spent his time in writing and travelling. His major novels are *Crime and Punishment*, *The Idiot*, *The Devils* and *The Brothers Karamazov*.

# John Dryden

All human things are subject to decay,
And, when fate summons, monarchs must obey.

*Mac Flecknoe*

None but the brave deserves the fair.

*Alexander's Feast*

Happy the man, and happy he alone,
He who can call today his own:
He who, secure within, can say,
To-morrow do thy worst, for I have lived to-day.

*Translation of Horace*

John Dryden (1631 – 1700) was born at Aldwinkle, North-ants, and went to London in 1657. In 1659 he published *Heroic Stanzas* in memory of Oliver Cromwell, but he hastened to celebrate the Restoration with *Astraea Redux*. He produced many plays and much other work, but at the Revolution of 1688 was deprived of the laureateship to which he had been appointed in 1668 because he was a Roman Catholic. Dryden was the greatest literary figure of his age.


# Marie Jeanne Becu Du Barry

After all, the world is but an amusing theatre, and I see no reason why a pretty woman should not play a principal part in it.

We learn to howl in the society of wolves.

Marie Jeanne Becu Du Barry (1743 – 93), daughter of a dressmaker, married the Comte Guillaume Du Barry and was presented at Court, where she soon became Mistress of Louis XV of France. She is said to have been strikingly handsome, not without wit, and frank to the point of vulgarity. She exercised great influence on Louis, but on his death she was banished to a convent. At the Revolution she fled to London, but returned to Paris in 1793, when she was arrested and guillotined.

# Thomas Alva Edison

Genius is one per cent inspiration and ninety-nine per cent perspiration.

*Newspaper interview in Life,*
*1932*

As a cure for worrying, work is better than whisky.

Thomas Alva Edison (1847–1931), American electrician and inventor, was born at Milan, Ohio, of mixed Dutch and Scottish descent. In early life a telegraph operator, he became Superintendent of the Law Gold Indicator Company. His inventive genius soon showed itself in the series of experiments into the improvement of electrical transmission, and he played a large part in the development of incandescent lamps, electric lighting and electric railways.

# Jonathan Edwards

The bodies of those that made such a noise and tumult when alive, when dead, lie as quietly among the graves of their neighbours as any others.

*Procrastination*

Jonathan Edwards (1703–58) was a New England philosopher and an ardent divine and formidable preacher. His principal philosophical work *A Careful and Strict Enquiry into the Modern Prevailing Notions of ... Freedom of Will* caused Johnson to say 'All theory is against freedom of the will; all experience for it'.

# Albert Einstein

If A is success in life, then A equals X plus Y plus Z. Work is X; Y is play; and Z is keeping your mouth shut.

I also am a revolutionary, though only a scientific one.

Professor Albert Einstein (1879 – 1955), a German–Swiss physicist, was the framer of the theories of relativity. After teaching at the Polytechnic School in Zurich he became a Swiss citizen and was appointed an inspector of patents at

Berne. In his spare time he obtained his PhD at Zurich, and some of his papers on physics were of such a high standard that in 1909 he was given a chair of theoretical physics at the University. His first theory – the so-called special theory of relativity – published in 1905, but in 1915 he issued his general theory. He received the Nobel Prize for physics in 1921 for his work in quantum theory.

## George Eliot

You love the roses – so do I. I wish
The sky would rain down roses, as they rain
From off the shaken bush...
... Why will it not?
Then all the valley would be pink and white
And soft to tread on.

*The Book of a Thousand*
*Poems, Roses*

George Eliot (1819–80) was the pseudonym of the British writer Mary Ann Evans. Born at Chilvers Coton, Warwickshire, she received a strictly evangelical upbringing but later moved to Coventry and was converted to free thinking. She became famous for her novels *Adam Bede*, *The Mill on the Floss* and *Silas Marner*, which were all set in her native county. Other novels followed; *Middlemarch* is regarded as her finest work and one of the greatest novels of the century.

## Elizabeth 1, Queen of England

If thy heart fails thee, climb not at all.

*Lines written on a window*
*after Sir Walter Raleigh's*
*own 'Fain would I climb, yet*
*fear to fall'*

I know I have the body of a weak and feeble woman, but I have the heart and stomach of a king, and of a king of England too.

*Speech to the Troops at*
*Tilbury on the approach of the*
*Armada, 1588*

Elizabeth 1 (1533–1603), Queen of England and the daughter of Henry VIII and Anne Boleyn, was born at Greenwich. During Mary's reign Elizabeth's Protestant sympathies brought her under suspicion, and she lived at Hatfield until she became Queen in 1558. Her reign lasted forty-five years, and its glories are one of the main themes of English history.

## Dame Edith Evans

As a young actress I always had a rule. If I didn't understand anything, I always said it as if it were improper.

*Quoted by Robin May in 'The Wit of the Theatre'*

Dame Edith Evans (1888–1976), the British actress, was well known for her versatility on the stage, but is famous for her portrayal of Lady Bracknell in *The Importance of Being Earnest*. She appeared in Shakespeare, Restoration comedy, Wilde and Shaw, as well as in films.

## David Everett

Don't view me with a critic's eye,
But pass my imperfections by.
Large streams from little fountains flow,
Tall oaks from little acorns grow.

*Lines written for a School Declamation*

David Everett (1770–1813) was an American author. Born in Princetown, Massachusetts, he became a lawyer and journalist, and was the author of *Common Sense in Dishabille, Daranzel* (a play performed in 1798 and 1800) and several other works.

## Gracie Fields

People are always sending me pictures of their aspidistras.

*10.9.1978*

Gracie Fields (1898–1979) was an English comedienne. Born Gracie Stansfield in Rochdale, she appeared in London in *Mr. Tower of London*, which gave over 4,000 performances. Later she became a popular motion-picture actress and singer.

## W.C. Fields

Smile first thing in the morning. Get it over with.

I'm allergic to water. My grandmother drowned in the filthy stuff.

*In Edgar Bergen's 'Chase and Sanborn Radio Show'*

In marriage a man must give up many of his old pleasant habits.

Marry an outdoors woman. Then if you throw her out into the yard for the night, she can still survive.

Never trust your wife behind your back, even if she claims she only wants to wash or scratch it.

Give a woman a hundred dollars in small bills and it won't last long. But a hundred dollar bill she'll hold on to for dear life. She'll keep postponing breaking it. Therefore you won't have to replenish her coffers for a long time.

*On the occasion of Carlotta Monti's birthday*

W.C. (Claude) Fields (1880–1946), was born in Philadelphia into a poor family named Dukinfield and ran away from home at the age of eleven. In July 1897 he obtained his first professional employment as a 'tramp juggler' in an open-air theatre near Norristown, Pennsylvania. Very soon afterwards he became a Vaudeville star on the Keith circuit.

## Henry Ford

History is bunk.

*In the witness box during his libel suit v the Chicago Tribune, July 1919*

You can have any colour you like, as long as it is black.

*When discussing the specification of his cars*

Luck and destiny are the excuses of the world's failures.

*6.3.1927*

Henry Ford (1863–1947), born at Greenfield, Michigan, developed an early interest in mechanics. He experimented in motorcar manufacture and started the business that grew into the Ford Motor Company, becoming for a time the largest maker of motorcars in the world. In 1914 he instituted a scheme of profit-sharing. With his son, Edsel, he engaged in tractor manufacture, and in 1940 set up the Willow Run bomber aircraft plant which became vital to the Allied war effort. The vehicle on which the fortunes of the Ford Motor Company were built was the 'Model T', introduced in 1909 and produced continuously until 1927, by which time more than fifteen million had been made.

## James Elroy Flecker

I have seen old ships sail like swans asleep
Beyond the village which men still call Tyre.

*The Old Ships*

Away, for we are ready to a man!
Our camels sniff the evening and are glad.
Lead on, O Master of the Caravan:
Lead on the Merchant Princes of Bagdad.

*The Golden Journey to Samarkand*

Have we not Indian carpets dark as wine,
Turbans and sashes, gowns and bows and veils,
And broideries of intricate design,
And printed hangings in enormous bales?

*The Golden Journey to Samarkand*

Sweet to ride forth at evening from the wells,
When shadows pass gigantic on the sand,
And softly through the silence beat the bells
Along the Golden Road to Samarkand.

*The Golden Journey to Samarkand*

James Elroy Flecker (1884–1915) entered the Consular service and was posted first to Constantinople and then to Beirut. He published *The Bridge of Fire*, *Forty-Two Poems*, *The Golden Journey to Samarkand* and *The Old Ships*. Two plays, *Hassan* and *Don Juan*, were published posthumously.

## Michael Foot

I had better recall, before someone else does, that I said on one occasion that all was fair in love, war, and parliamentary procedure.

*7.9.1975*

More Governments, including left-wing Governments, have been thrown out of power through a failure to deal with inflation than through any other single cause.

*18.4.1978*

What politics is all about is to try to combine protection of your principles with effective action. It is no use having effective action if you do not protect your principles.

*On being voted Leader of the
Labour Party, 10.11.1980*

The Right Hon Michael Foot (1913–), son of the late Sir Isaac Foot, has been MP for Ebbw Vale since 1960. He became Deputy Leader of the Labour Party in 1976 and was voted Leader of the Opposition upon the resignation of James Callaghan in 1980. He held the post of assistant editor of the *Tribune* in 1937/8, was acting editor of the *Evening Standard* in 1942, and political columnist of the *Daily Herald* from 1944 until 1964.

## St Francis of Assissi

Lord, make us instruments of thy peace. Where there is hatred, let us sow love; where there is injury, pardon; where there is discord, union; where there is doubt, faith; where there is despair, hope; where there is darkness, light; where there is sadness, joy.

St Francis of Assissi (1162–1226) was the son of a wealthy Italian merchant. In his early twenties he gave away all his wealth and took up a life of poverty and service, which attracted many followers. Many stories are told of his ability to charm wild animals and to influence men in all walks of life.

## Robert Frost

Home is the place where, when you have to go there, they have to take you in.

A poem begins in delight and ends in wisdom.

All men are born free and equal – free at least in their right to be different. Some people want to homogenize society everywhere. I'm against the homogenizers in art, in politics, in every walk of life. I want the cream to rise.

*The Letters of Robert Frost to*
*Louis Untermeyer*

Robert Lee Frost (1874 – 1963) was an American poet. Born in San Francisco, he farmed unsuccessfully in New Hampshire, but combined it with teaching and writing poetry. He sailed to England and established his reputation as the author of several books, then returned to America and won Pulitzer poetry prizes for *New Hampshire*, *Collected Poems*, *A Further Range* and *A Witness Tree*.

## Zsa Zsa Gabor

Never despise what it says in the women's magazines; it may not be subtle, but neither are men.

Zsa Zsa Gabor (1919–) was born Sari Gabor. This glamorous international lady was Miss Hungary of 1936. She has since appeared in films of many nations, including *Lovely to Look At* (USA), *Lily* (USA), *Moulin Rouge* (GB), *Public Enemy Number One* (France) and *Diary of a Scoundrel* (USA).

## Paul Getty

My formula for success? Rise early, work late, strike oil. If all the money and property in the world were divided up equally at say, three o'clock in the afternoon, by 3.30 there would already be notable differences in the financial conditions of the recipients. Within that first thirty minutes, some adults would have lost their share, some would have gambled theirs away, and some would have been swindled or cheated out of their portion, thereby making some others richer...

... The disparity would increase with growing momentum as time went on. After ninety days the difference would be staggering. And I'm willing to wager that, within a year or two at the most, the distribution of wealth would conform to patterns almost identical with those that had previously prevailed.

*From his autobiography 'As I See It'*

John Paul Getty (1892–1976) was an American oil millionaire. He was President of the Getty Oil Co from 1947 and founder of the J. Paul Getty Museum, California, which is noted for its eighteenth-century French furniture and tapestries, and an art collection ranging through the fifteenth to seventeenth centuries.

## W.S. Gilbert

When I was a lad I served a term
As office-boy to an Attorney's firm.
I cleaned the windows and I swept the floor,
And I polished up the handle of the big front door.

*HMS Pinafore*

Sir William Schwenk Gilbert (1836 – 1911), the British humorist and dramatist, collaborated with Sir Arthur Sullivan in a great series of comic-operas, the popularity of them being due as much to Gilbert's lyrics as to Sullivan's music. Unfortunately, the personal relationship between the two men became cool, and the partnership broke down owing to temperamental incompatability.

## Johann Wolfgang von Goethe

It is not doing the thing we like to do, but liking the thing we have to do, that makes life blessed.

Give me the benefit of your convictions if you have any; but keep your doubts to yourself, for I have enough of my own.

Know you the land where the lemon-trees bloom?
In the dark foliage the golden oranges glow; a soft wind hovers from the sky, the myrtle is still and the laurel stands tall.

*Wilhelm Meisters Lehrjahre*

Johann Wolfgang Von Goethe (1749–1832), the German poet and man of letters, statesman and natural philosopher, discovered his poetic vocation while studying law at Leipzig. He met Herder at Strasbourg and became leader of the Storm and Stress movement. Later he moved to Weimar and entered the service of Duke Karl August. The first part of his *Faust* appeared in 1808, but the second part was not published until 1831.

## Oliver Goldsmith

When lovely woman stoops to folly,
And finds too late that men betray,
What charm can soothe her melancholy,
What art can wash her guilt away?

*The Vicar of Wakefield*

Sweet Auburn! loveliest village of the plain.

*The Deserted Village*

A man he was to all the country dear,
And passing rich with forty pounds a year.

*The Deserted Village*

Here lies David Garrick, describe me, who can,
An abridgement of all that was pleasant in man.

*Retaliation*

On the stage he was natural, simple, affecting;
'Twas only that when he was off he was acting [Garrick].

*Retaliation*

I love everything that's old; old friends, old times, old manners, old books, old wines.

*She Stoops to Conquer*

Oliver Goldsmith (1728–74) was born in Ireland, the son of a clergyman. He was educated at Trinity College, Dublin, then went to Edinburgh to study medicine. Later he went abroad and wandered through France, Switzerland and Italy, then returned to England and wrote his *History of England* and *Animated Nature*. Upon meeting Johnson he became a member of his 'Club', established his reputation with his poem *The Traveller*, and followed it with some collected essays, *The Vicar of Wakefield*, *The Deserted Village* and *She Stoops to Conquer*.

## Samuel Goldwyn

Anyone who visits a psychiatrist wants his head examined.

Why should people go out to see bad films when they can stay at home and see bad television?

The reason so many people showed up at Louis B. Mayer's funeral was because they wanted to make sure he was dead.

Going to call him William? What kind of a name is that? Every Tom, Dick and Harry's called William. Why don't you call him Bill?

Yes, my wife's hands are very beautiful. I'm going to have a bust made of them.

If you can't give me your word of honour, will you give me your promise?

Samuel Goldwyn (1882–1974) was born of Jewish parents in Warsaw. As a Pole with an unpronounceable name, he arrived in the United States, and an immigration official named him 'Goldfish'. Eventually he realised the trick that had been played on him and changed it to Goldwyn. He founded the Goldwyn Pictures Corporation which later became the Metro-Goldwyn-Mayer Company in 1925. He is particularly famed for his witty sayings or 'Goldwynisms'.

## Kenneth Grahame

Believe me, my young friend, there is *nothing* – absolutely nothing – half so much worth doing as simply messing about in boats.

*The Wind in the Willows*

The clever men at Oxford
Know all that there is to be knowed.
But they none of them know one half as much
As intelligent Mr. Toad.

*The Wind in the Willows*

Kenneth Grahame (1859–1932) was born in Edinburgh, son of an advocate, and worked at the Bank of England from 1878 to 1908. His early volumes of sketches of childhood – *The Golden Age* and *Dream Days* – were followed by his masterpiece *The Wind in the Willows*, an animal fantasy originally created for his little son. It became a successful stage play in A.A. Milne's dramatisation as *Toad of Toad Hall*.


## Thomas Gray

The curfew tolls the knell of parting day,
The lowing herd winds slowly o'er the lea,
The ploughman homeward plods his weary way,
And leaves the world to darkness and to me.

*Elegy written in a Country*
*Churchyard*

Full many a flower is born to blush unseen,
And waste its sweetness on the desert air.

*Elegy written in a Country*
*Churchyard*

Not all that tempts your wand'ring eyes
And heedless hearts, is lawful prize;
Nor all that glisters, gold.

*Ode on the Death of a*
*Favourite Cat*

… Where ignorance is bliss
'Tis folly to be wise.

*Ode on a Distant Prospect of*
*Eton College*

Thomas Gray (1716–71) was born in London. At Eton he formed a close friendship with Horace Walpole and together they went on a tour of France and Italy. Upon his return, Gray lived again in London, but visited his mother and sister at Stoke Poges. For some time he wrote poems which appeared anonymously in Dodsley's *Miscellany*, but in 1750 he wrote the now famous *Elegy written in a Country Churchyard*. The location was presumed to be Stoke Poges.

## Joyce Grenfell

If I should go before the rest of you
Break not a flower nor inscribe a stone,
Nor when I'm gone speak in a Sunday voice
But be the usual selves that I have known.

*Quoted in 'Radio Times'*
*1.1.1981*

Weep if you must,
Parting is hell,
But life goes on,
So sing as well.

*Quoted in 'Radio Times'*
*1.1.1981*

Joyce Grenfell (1910–79), comedienne, film-star, expert at writing and speaking monologues, panellist on Joseph Cooper's 'Face the Music' programmes – Joyce Grenfell was all this and much more. Her books very quickly became bestsellers, and gave the fascinating story of her life.

## Sir Edward Grey

The lamps are going out all over Europe; we shall not see them lit again in our lifetime.

Sir Edward Grey (First Viscount of Fallodon, 1862–1933) was the eldest son of Captain George Henry Grey. He was educated at Winchester and Balliol College, Oxford, and from 1895 was Under-Secretary for Foreign Affairs. From 1885 to 1916 he was MP for Berwick-on-Tweed, and was created Viscount of Fallodon in 1916.

## François Guizot

Do not be afraid of enthusiasm. You need it. You can do nothing effectually without it.

François Pierre Guillaume Guizot (1787–1874) was a French statesman and historian. Born at Nîmes, he was a Protestant and from 1812 to 1830 was professor of history at the Sorbonne. He wrote about the history of civilisation and became Prime Minister in 1847.

## Joseph Hall

Moderation is the silken string running through the pearl chain of all virtues.

*Christian Moderation,*
*Introduction*

Joseph Hall (1574–1656) was Bishop of Exeter and Norwich. Educated at Ashby-de-la-Zouch and Emmanuel College, Cambridge, he published some satires which were attacked by Marston in 1601. He became chaplain to Henry, Prince of Wales, and chaplain to Lord Doncaster in France; also he accompanied James I to Scotland. Impeached and imprisoned in 1642, he had his episcopal revenues sequestered in 1643 and was expelled from his palace in 1647.

## Oscar Hammerstein II

A sudden beam of moonlight, or a thrush you have just heard, or a girl you have just kissed, or a beautiful view through your study window is seldom the source of an urge to put words on paper. Such pleasant experiences are likely to obstruct and delay a writer's work.

Oscar Hammerstein II (1895–1960) was an immensely successful lyricist who wrote many stage musicals, usually with Richard Rodgers. Together they achieved fame with such shows as *The King and I*, *South Pacific* and *The Sound of Music*, and are well remembered for such songs as *Oh What a Beautiful Morning* and *Younger than Springtime*.

## Thomas Hardy

This is the weather the cuckoo likes,
And so do I:
When showers betumble the chestnut spikes
And nestlings fly;
And the little brown nightingale bills his best,
And they sit outside at the 'Traveller's Rest'.

*Weathers*

And maids come forth sprig-muslin drest,
And citizens dream of the south and west,
And so do I.

*Weathers*

Sweet cyder is a great thing,
A great thing to me,
Spinning down to Weymouth town
By Ridgway thirstily,
And maid and mistress summoning,
Who tend the hostelry –

*Great Things*

Thomas Hardy (1840 – 1928) became widely known and acclaimed as the Wessex author. Born at Bockhampton near Dorchester, he wrote *Far From the Madding Crowd* and *Under the Greenwood Tree* there before moving away and writing *The Return of the Native, The Mayor of Casterbridge* and others, including his famous *Tess of the D'Urbervilles*. He also wrote many poems.

## Joel Chandler Harris

Oh, whar shill we go w'en de great day comes,
Wid de blowin' er de trumpits en de bangin' er de drums?
How many po' sinners'll be kotched out late
En find no latch ter de golden gate?

*Uncle Remus, His Songs*

Joel Chandler Harris (1848 – 1908), the American writer, was born in Georgia and first published his *Uncle Remus* stories in the Atlanta *Constitution* which he edited from 1890 to 1905. The tales were written in Negro dialect and gained worldwide popularity. His autobiography *On the Plantation* was published in 1892.

## Minnie Louise Haskins

And I said to the man who stood at the gate of the year: 'Give me a light that I may tread safely into the unknown'. And he replied: 'Go out into the darkness and put your hand into the hand of God. That shall be to you better than light and safer than a known way.'

*From 'God Knows', quoted by*
*King George VI in his*
*Christmas broadcast on 25*
*December 1939*

Minnie Louise Haskins (1875–1957) was educated at Clarendon College, Clifton, the London School of Economics and the University of London. For some years she did educational work in India, and in the First World War.

## William Hazlitt

Give me the clear blue sky over my head, and the green turf beneath my feet, a winding road before me, and a three hours' march to dinner.

*Table Talk*

The rule for travelling abroad is to take our common sense with us, and leave our prejudices behind.

*Table Talk*

William Hazlitt (1778–1830) dabbled in portrait painting, but took to writing on the advice of Coleridge. He then went to London where he contributed to the press and various magazines. He became famous for, amongst other works, *Table Talk* and *The Spirit of the Age*.

## Edward Heath

We must recapture our European voice, the voice all of us instinctively realise, a voice of reason, of humanity, of moderation, which can be heard throughout the world.

*22.10.1972*

If politicians lived on praise and thanks, they'd be forced into some other line of business.

*30.9.1973*

I have told the country before that capitalism has its unacceptable face. If you want to see the acceptable face of capitalism, go out to an oil-rig in the North Sea.

*24.2.1974*

The crunch, so long awaited, so often discussed, is now upon us.

*10.10.1976*

Edward Heath (1916–) was leader of the Conservative Party from 1965–75; he became Prime Minister in 1970, remaining in that office until 1974, and was Leader of the Opposition from 1974–5. His unswerving faith in European unity was rewarded in 1972 by Britain's successful application for entry into the European Economic Community. His premiership from 1970 to 1974 was marked by bitter confrontation with the Unions. In the contest for the leadership of the Conservative Party held in February 1975, he was defeated in the first ballot by Mrs Thatcher and did not contest the second.

## Felicia Dorothea Hemans

The boy stood on the burning deck
Whence all but he had fled;
The flame that lit the battle's wreck
Shone round him o'er the dead.

*Casabianca*

There came a burst of thunder sound –
The boy – oh, where was he?

*Casabianca*

The stately homes of England,
How beautiful they stand!
Amidst their tall ancestral trees,
O'er all the pleasant land.

*The Homes of England*

Felicia Dorothea Hemans (1793–1835), a British poet, was born in Liverpool. She published many volumes of sentimental verse which attained great popularity, but her best-known poem is *Casabianca*.

# William Ernest Henley

It matters not how strait the gate,
How charged with punishments the scroll,
I am the master of my fate:
I am the captain of my soul.

> *Echoes: Invictus. In Memoriam of*
> *R.T. Hamilton Bruce*

Under the bludgeonings of chance
My head is bloody, but unbowed.

> *Echoes: Invictus. In Memoriam of*
> *R.T. Hamilton Bruce*

A late lark twitters from the quiet skies.

> *Echoes: In Memoriam of*
> *Margaritae Sororis*

What have I done for you,
England, my England?
What is there I would not do,
England, my own?

> *For England's Sake, iii. Pro Rege Nostro*

William Ernest Henley (1849–1903) was born at Gloucester. Tuberculosis and the subsequent amputation of a left
leg left him crippled from boyhood. He wrote much
verse, criticism and miscellaneous journalism, and was
closely associated with Stevenson, with whom he wrote
*Deacon Brodie* and other plays.

# Robert Herrick

I sing of brooks, of blossoms, birds and bowers;
Of April, May, of June and July flowers

> *Hesperides: The Argument of His Book*

Gather ye rosebuds while ye may
Old Time is still a-flying...

> *Hesperides: To the Virgins*

Robert Herrick (1591–1674) was born in Cheapside,
London, and was a friend of Ben Jonson. In 1629 he
became vicar of Dean Prior, near Totnes, and in 1648
published *Hesperides*, which was a collection of sacred
and pastoral poetry of unrivalled lyric quality.

## Paul Hindemith

People who make music together cannot be enemies, at least not while the music lasts.

*A Composer's World*

Paul Hindemith (1895–1963) was a German composer. A fine viola player, he led the Frankfurt Opera Orchestra at twenty, and taught composition at the Berlin Hochschule for Music from 1927 to 1933, when the modernity of his *Philharmonic Concerto* led to a Nazi ban. In 1939 he went to America where he taught at Yale and in 1952 he became professor of musical theory at Zurich.

## Alfred Hitchcock

Suspense is a matter of knowledge. If a bomb unexpectedly goes off in a film – that's surprise. But if the audience knows a bomb will go off in five minutes, and the hero on screen doesn't know it – that's suspense.

Alfred Hitchcock (1899–1981) was a British film director and a master of suspense. His notable films include *The Thirty-nine Steps, Rebecca, Rope, Strangers on a Train, Rear Window, Vertigo, Psycho* and *The Birds*.

## Oliver Wendell Holmes

Nine times out of ten, the first thing a man's companion knows of his short-comings is from his apology.

If I had a formula for bypassing trouble, I would not pass it round. Trouble creates a capacity to handle it. I don't embrace trouble; that's as bad as treating it as an enemy. But I do say meet it as a friend, for you'll see a lot of it and had better be on speaking terms with it.

Oliver Wendell Holmes (1809–94) was an American writer. Born in Cambridge, Massachusetts, he became professor of anatomy at Dartmouth and later at Harvard. Later still with Lowell he founded the *Atlantic Monthly* and published *The Professor at the Breakfast Table*.

# Thomas Hood

Never go to France
Unless you know the lingo.
If you do, like me,
You will repent, by jingo.

*Family Word Finder*

Thomas Hood (1799–1845) was a British poet. Born in London, he entered journalism and edited periodicals which included *Hood's Magazine*. Best known for his comic verse, he also wrote serious poems such as *Song of the Shirt* and *Bridge of Sighs*.

# Horace

He who has begun his task has half done it.

*Epistles*

If you do not know how to live aright, make way for those who do ... It is time for you to leave the scene.

*Epistles*

What shall be to-morrow, think not of asking. Each day that Fortune gives you, be it what it may, set down for gain.

*Odes*

The snows have scattered and fled; already the grass comes again in the fields and the leaves on the trees.

*Odes*

Quintus Horatius Flaccus Horace (65–8BC), the Roman poet, was born at Venusia in Apulia and was present on the losing side at the battle of Philippi, but obtained his pardon and returned to Rome. He was given a Sabine farm and then wrote poems which included *Satires*, *Odes*, *Epistles* and the *Ars Poetica*.

# Sir Fred Hoyle

Outer space isn't remote at all. It's only an hour's drive away if your car could go straight upward.

Sir Fred Hoyle (1915–), the British astronomer, was educated at Cambridge and became Plumian professor of astronomy and experimental philosophy there in 1958. He became famous for his radio talks and science fiction as well as his contribution to cosmological theory (continuous creation) and such books as *Nuclei* and *Quasars*.

## Victor Hugo

Common-sense is in spite of, not the result of, education.

Victor Marie Hugo (1802–85) was a French poet, novelist and dramatist. Born at Besançon, the son of one of Napoleon's generals, he established himself as the leader of French Romanticism with the verse play *Hernani*. Later plays included *Lucrece Borgia*. In 1851 he was banished for opposing Louis Napoleon's coup d'état and settled in Guernsey, but on the fall of the Empire in 1870 he returned to France and became a senator.

## T.H. Huxley

The rung of a ladder was never meant to rest upon, but only to hold a man's foot long enough to enable him to put the other somewhat higher.

Thomas Henry Huxley (1825–95) was a British scientist, humanist and agnostic thinker. Born at Ealing, he graduated in medicine and for several years was surgeon to *HMS Rattlesnake* on a surveying expedition in the South Seas. Following the publication of *The Origin of Species* in 1859, he won fame as 'Darwin's bulldog', and for many years was the most prominent and popular champion of evolution.

## Jerome K. Jerome

Love is like the measles; we all have to go through it.
*Idle Thoughts of an Idle*
*Fellow, On Being in Love*

I like work; it fascinates me. I can sit and look at it for hours. I love to keep it by me: the idea of getting rid of it nearly breaks my heart.

*Three Men in a Boat*

Jerome Klapka Jerome (1859–1927), after being educated in London, became a clerk and a teacher. In 1885 he published *On the Stage and Off*, then made his name with *Three Men in a Boat*. This was followed by *Idle Thoughts of an Idle Fellow* and several novels. Jerome K. Jerome wrote many plays, the best known of which is probably *The Passing of the Third Floor Back*.

## Samuel Johnson

Prepare for death if here at night you roam,
And sign your will before you sup from home.

*London*

I am not yet so lost in lexicography, as to forget that words are the daughters of earth, and that things are the sons of heaven.

*Preface: Dictionary of the English Language*

A man, Sir, should keep his friendship in constant repair.

*Letter to Lord Chesterfield, 1755*

Depend upon it, Sir, when a man knows he is to be hanged in a fortnight, it concentrates his mind wonderfully.

*Letter to Lord Chesterfield*

Kindness is generally reciprocal; we are desirous of pleasing others because we receive pleasure from them.

Adversity is the state in which a man most easily becomes acquainted with himself, being especially free from admirers then.

My master whipt me very well. Without that, Sir, I should have done nothing! While Hunter was flogging the boys unmercifully, he used to say – 'And this I do to save you from the gallows.'

61

There is no private house in which people can enjoy themselves as well as in a capital tavern. Let there be ever so much elegance, ever so much desire that everybody should be easy; in the nature of things it cannot be; there must be some degree of care and anxiety...

The master of the house is anxious to entertain his guests; the guests are anxious to be agreeable to him; and no man, but a very impudent dog indeed, can so freely command what is in another man's house, as if it were his own...

Whereas, at a tavern, there is a general freedom from anxiety. You are sure you are welcome; and the more noise you make, the more trouble you give, the more good things you call for, the welcomer you are...

No servants will attend you with the alacrity which waiters do, who are excited by the prospect of an immediate reward in proportion as they please ...

*On Inns*

Samuel Johnson (1709–84) was an English lexicographer, author and critic. Born in Lichfield, he was educated at Lichfield Grammar School and Pembroke College, Oxford. He entered the service of Edward Cave the printer and in 1747 issued the 'plan' of his *Dictionary* for Lord Chesterfield's consideration but it was not published until 1755. Johnson was one of the founders of the Literary Club in Fleet Street, and it was there that he became so closely associated with James Boswell, his biographer.

## Joseph Joubert

What is left of human wisdom after age has purified it may be the best we have.

One should chose for a wife only a woman one would choose for a friend if she were a man.

A clever talk between two men is a unison: between a man and a woman it is harmony: we come away satisfied by one, enchanted by the other.

He who has no poetry in himself will find poetry in nothing.

We must respect the past and mistrust the present if we are to safeguard the future.

It is better to turn over a question without deciding it than to decide it without turning it over.

The evening of life comes bearing its own lamp.

Joseph Joubert (1754–1824) was a French thinker and is famous for his posthumously published work *Pensees*, *Essais Maximes* and *Correspondance*.

## Yousuf Karsh

Great men are often lonely. But perhaps that loneliness is part of their ability to create. Character, like a photograph, develops in darkness.

Yousuf Karsh (1908–), the Canadian photographer, was born in Armenia. He made use of strong highlights and shadows, and in 1933 opened his own studio in Ottawa. His 'bulldog' portrait of Churchill in the Second World War brought him world fame.

## John Keats

Season of mists and mellow fruitfulness,
Close bosom-friend of the maturing sun.

*To Autumn*

To bend with apples the moss'd cottage-trees,
And fill all fruit with ripeness to the core.

*To Autumn*

A thing of beauty is a joy forever:
Its loveliness increases.

*Endymion*

I cannot see what flowers are at my feet,
Nor what soft incense hangs upon the boughs.

*To a Nightingale*

'Beauty is truth, truth beauty,' – that is all
Ye know on earth, and all ye need to know.

*On a Grecian Urn*

And there shall be for thee all soft delight.

*To Psyche*

John Keats (1795–1821) was the son of a livery-stable keeper in London. He acquired a knowledge of Latin and history, and some French, was apprenticed to a surgeon and became a student at Guy's Hospital. However he soon abandoned medicine for poetry and was at first not very successful. Later he wrote *Endymion, The Eve of St. Agnes, La Belle Dame sans Merci* and the unfinished *Eve of St. Mark.* About the same time he wrote his great odes *On a Grecian Urn, To a Nightingale* and *To Autumn,* as well as odes *On Melancholy, On Indolence* and *To Psyche.*

## Helen Keller

Security does not exist in nature, nor do the children of men as a whole experience it. Avoiding danger is no safer in the long run than exposure. Life is either a daring adventure or nothing.

*On Security*

With my three trusty guides, touch, smell and taste, I make many excursions into the borderland of experience... Nature accommodates itself to every man's necessity. If the eye is maimed, so that it does not see the beauteous face of the day, the touch becomes more poignant and discriminating. Nature proceeds through practice to strengthen and augment the remaining senses.

*Life with Three Senses, The*
*World I Live In*

When we do the best that we can, we never know what miracle is wrought in our life or in the life of another.

Helen Adams Keller (1880 – 1968) was an American author who became famous because of her great triumph over adversity. At only nineteen months old she suffered an illness through which she lost the senses of sight and hearing, and consequently became dumb. After a painful period of frustration she was helped by the skill and patience of Anne Sullivan Macy, who taught her how to speak. Under Anne's expert guidance Helen Keller graduated with honours at Radcliffe College in 1904, and later published several books. Her first meeting with her teacher was described in William Gibson's play *The Miracle Worker* (1959) which was made into a film in 1962.

## Lord Kilmuir

When the ruins of Pompeii were uncovered, dice were found. It is a sad commentary on the unvarying conditions of human nature that some of the dice were loaded.
*Sayings of the Week*

Lord Kilmuir (David Patrick Maxwell Fife, 1900–67), British lawyer and Conservative politician, was called to the Bar in 1922. He became an MP in 1935, Solicitor-General from 1942–5 and Attorney General in 1945 during the Churchill governments. At the Nuremberg trials he was deputy to Sir Hartley Shawcross and for most of the time conducted the British prosecution. He was Home Secretary from 1951 to 1954 and Lord Chancellor from 1954 to 1962. In 1954 he was created Viscount and in 1962 Earl.

## Martin Luther King

I have a dream that one day on the red hills of Georgia, the sons of former slaves and the sons of former slave-owners will be able to sit down together at the table of brotherhood.
*Speech at Civil Rights March*
*on Washington, 28 August 1963*

I have a dream that my four little children will one day live in a nation where they will not be judged by the colour of their skin, but by the content of their character.
*Speech at Civil Rights March*
*on Washington, 28 August 1963*

Injustice anywhere is a threat to justice everywhere.
*Letter from Birmingham Alabama Jail,*
*published in the Atlantic Monthly, August 1963*

I just want to do God's will. And he's allowed me to go to the mountain. And I've looked over, and I've seen the promised land... So I'm happy tonight. I'm not worried about anything. I'm not fearing any man.

*Speech at Birmingham*
*Alabama on 3 April 1968, the*
*evening before his*
*assassination*

Martin Luther King (1929–68) was an eloquent black Baptist minister who, from the middle 1950s until his assassination in April 1968, led the first mass civil rights movement in United States history. He achieved world-wide recognition when he was awarded the 1964 Nobel Prize for Peace for his application of the principle of non-violent resistance – patterned after India's Mahatma Gandhi – in the struggle for racial equality in America.

## Rudyard Kipling

Oh, East is East, and West is West, and never the twain shall meet,
Till Earth and Sky stand presently at God's great Judgment Seat;
But there is neither East nor West, Border, nor Breed nor Birth,
When two strong men stand face to face, though they come from the ends of the earth.

*The Ballad of East and West*

Teach us delight in simple things,
And mirth that has no bitter springs:
Forgiveness free of evil done,
And love to all men 'neath the sun.

*The Children's Song*

Our England is a garden, that is full of stately views,
Of borders, beds and shrubberies and lawns and avenues,
With statues on the terraces and peacocks strutting by;
But the glory of the Garden lies in more than meets the eye.

*The Glory of the Garden*

'Oh, where are you going to, all you Big Steamers,
With England's own coal, up and down the salt seas?'
'We are going to fetch you your bread and your butter,
Your beef, pork, and mutton, eggs, apples, and cheese.'

*Big Steamers*

Rudyard Kipling (1865–1936) was the son of John Lockwood Kipling, the illustrator of *Beast and Man in India*. He was born in Bombay, educated at the United Services College, Westward Ho! and engaged in journalistic work in India between 1882 and 1889. His fame rests largely on his short stories which dealt with India, the sea, the jungle and its beasts, the army and the navy. Kipling is best known for his two *Jungle Books, Kim, The Just-So Stories, Puck of Pook's Hill* and *Stalky and Co.* and he was awarded the Nobel Prize for Literature in 1907.

## La Bruyère

Modesty is to merit what shadow is to the figures in a picture; it gives accent and strength.

Every vice falsely resembles some virtue, and it always takes advantage of the resemblance.

There is no trade in the world so toilsome as that of pursuing fame; life is over before the main part of your work has begun.

There are but three events which concern mankind; birth, life, and death. All know nothing of their birth, all submit to die, and many forget to live.

Jean de La Bruyère (1645–96), a French essayist, was born in Paris, studied law, took a post in the Revenue office, and in 1684 entered the service of the house of Condé. His *Caractères* (satirical portraits of contemporaries) made him many enemies.

# La Rochefoucauld

If we cannot find peace within ourselves, it is useless to look for it elsewhere.

Passion often turns the cleverest man into an idiot and the greatest blockhead into someone clever.

It takes greater character to handle good fortune than bad.

Self-interest blinds some people and sharpens the eyesight of others.

To establish yourself in the world, do all you can to seem established already.

Francois, Duc de la Rochefoucauld (1613–80) was born in Paris, became a soldier and took part in the wars of the Fronde. His later years were divided between the Court and literary society. He is best known for his work *Réflexions, Sentences et Maximes Morales* (1665).

# Emma Lazarus

Give me your tired, your poor,
Your huddled masses yearning to be free,
The wretched refuse of your teeming shore,
Send these, the homeless, tempest-tossed, to me;
I lift my lamp beside the golden door.

*Lines inscribed on the Statue of Liberty*

Emma Lazarus (1849–87), an American poet, essayist and philanthropist, was born in New York City. She published a number of works, including *Alide; An Episode of Goethe's Life* in 1874. She championed oppressed Jews during persecution in Russia, and wrote *Songs of a Semite*.

# Stephen Leacock

Many a man in love with a dimple makes the mistake of marrying the whole girl.

Writing is not hard. Just get paper and pencil, sit down and write it as it occurs to you. The writing is easy – it's the occurring that's hard.

Stephen Leacock (1869–1944), a British humorous writer born in Hampshire, lived in Canada from 1876 and became head of the department of economics at McGill University, Montreal, from 1908 until 1936. He published works on politics and economics, and studies of Mark Twain and Dickens, but is best known for his humorous writings. These include *Literary Lapses*, *Nonsense Novels* and *Frenzied Fiction*.

## Edward Lear

'How pleasant to know Mr. Lear!'
Who has written such volumes of stuff!
Some think him ill-tempered and queer,
But a few think him pleasant enough.

*Nonsense Songs: Preface*

On the coast of Coromandel
Where the early pumpkins blow,
In the middle of the woods
Lived the Yonghy-Bonghy-Bò.
Two old chairs, and half a candle, –
One old jug without a handle, –
These were all his wordly goods.

*Nonsense Songs: The
Courtship of the
Yonghy-Bonghy-Bò*

Edward Lear (1812–88), the British artist and humorist, first attracted attention with his paintings of birds, but later turned to painting landscapes. He travelled in Italy, Greece, Egypt and India and published books on his travels with his own illustrations. He published his *Book of Nonsense* in 1846, which he illustrated himself, and popularized the limerick.

## C.S. Lewis

Friendship is born at the moment when one person says to another, 'What! You too? I thought I was the only one.'

Reality is usually something you could not have guessed. That is one of the reasons I believe Christianity. It is a religion you could not have guessed. If it offered us just the kind of universe we had always expected, I should feel we were making it up. It has just that queer twist about it that real things have.

Clive Staples Lewis (1898–1963) was a British scholar. From 1954 to 1963 he was professor of Medieval and Renaissance English at Cambridge, and his books include the remarkable medieval study *The Allegory of Love* and the science fiction *Out of the Silent Planet*. He also wrote some essays in popular theology, the autobiographical *Surprise by Joy*, and a number of books for children.

## Abraham Lincoln

In giving freedom to the slave we assure freedom to the free,—honourable alike in what we give and what we preserve.

*Annual Message to Congress,*
*1862*

That this nation, under God, shall have a new birth of freedom, and that government of the people, by the people, for the people, shall not perish from the earth.

*Address at Gettysburg, 1863*

I claim not to have controlled events, but confess plainly that events have controlled me.

*Letter to A.G. Hodges, 1864*

With malice towards none; with charity for all; with firmness in the right, as God gives us to see the right, let us strive on to finish the work we are in; to bind up the nation's wounds; to care for him who shall have borne the battle, and for his widow and his orphan—to do all which may achieve and cherish a just and lasting peace among ourselves and with all nations.

*Second Inaugural Address,*
*1865*

I don't know who my grandfather was. I am much more concerned to know what his grandson will be.

Abraham Lincoln (1809–65) was the sixteenth President of the USA. Born in a Kentucky log cabin, he was almost entirely self-educated but qualified as a lawyer. Entering politics, he sat first as a Whig, then joined the new Republican Party in 1856, and became President on a minority vote in 1860. Between his election and his inauguration seven slave states seceded from the Union, and these were followed by four more. Civil War soon raged and Lincoln became extremely unpopular. In 1863 his proclamation freed slaves in the Confederate territory. Five days after Robert E. Lee's surrender Lincoln was assassinated by a Confederate fanatic.

## David Lloyd George

Don't be afraid to take a big step if one is indicated. You can't cross a chasm in two small jumps.

David Lloyd George (1863–1945) was a Welsh Liberal statesman. Born in Manchester, the son of a teacher, he became an MP, making his reputation as a fiery Radical and Welsh Nationalist. The First World War brought him fame as the dominating figure in the Cabinet—he was Prime Minister of the Coalition Government in 1916—and after the war he was among those primarily responsible for the Versailles peace settlement.

## Henry Wadsworth Longfellow

Lives of great men all remind us
We can make our lives sublime,
And, departing, leave behind us
Footprints in the sands of time.

*A Psalm of Life*

Let us, then, be up and doing,
With a heart for any fate;
Still achieving, still pursuing,
Learn to labour and to wait.

*A Psalm of Life*

Ships that pass in the night, and speak each other in
passing;
Only a signal shown and a distant voice in the darkness;
So on the ocean of life we pass and speak one another,
Only a look and a voice; then darkness again and a
silence.

*Tales of a Wayside Inn, The*
*Theologian's Tale*

Then the little Hiawatha
Learned of every bird its language,
Learned their names and all their secrets,
How they built their nests in Summer,
Where they hid themselves in Winter,
Talked with them whene'er he met them,
Called them 'Hiawatha's chickens'.

*Hiawatha's Childhood*

Silently one by one, in the infinite meadows of heaven,
Blossomed the lovely stars, the forget-me-nots of the
angels.

*Evangeline*

The heights by great men reached and kept
Were not attained by sudden flight,
But they, while their companions slept,
Were toiling upward in the night.

*The Ladder of Saint*
*Augustine*

And the night shall be filled with music,
And the cares that infest the day,
Shall fold their tents like the Arabs,
And as silently steal away.

*The Day is Done*

Build me straight, O worthy Master!
Staunch and strong, a goodly vessel.

Thou, too, sail on, O Ship of State!

*The Building of the Ship*

Henry Wadsworth Longfellow (1807–82), the American
poet, published his first volume of poems *Voices in the
Night* in 1839 and *Ballads and Other Poems* in 1841.
These were soon followed by *Poems on Slavery, Hiawatha*

(1855), *The Courtship of Miles Standish* and *Tales of a Wayside Inn*.

## Anita Loos

Kissing your hand may make you feel very very good, but a diamond and sapphire bracelet lasts for ever.

*Gentlemen Prefer Blondes*

Anita Loos (1893–1981), the American humorist, collaborated with her husband in writing motion-picture scenarios, and was author of *Gentlemen Prefer Blondes* (1925) and *But Gentlemen Marry Brunettes* (1928).

## Samuel Lover

When once the itch of literature comes over a man, nothing can cure it but the scratching of a pen.

*Handy Andy*

Samuel Lover (1797–1868) was born in Dublin and became a painter of miniatures, but in 1835 he settled in London and conquered society by singing his own compositions. These he published as *Songs and Ballads*, but he is also remembered for his humorous novels *Rory O'More* and *Handy Andy*.

## Edward George Bulwer-Lytton

Beneath the rule of men entirely great
The pen is mightier than the sword.

*Richelieu*

Revolutions are not made with rose-water.

*The Parisians*

Edward George Earle Lytton Bulwer-Lytton (1803–73), first Baron Lytton, was born in London. His father was a soldier and his mother a member of the old family of Lytton. He published his first poems in 1820, and later his novels followed every turn of the public taste. He became famous for *Falkland*, *Eugene Aram* and *The Last Days of Pompeii*, and as a playwright achieved success with *Richelieu*.

## Thomas Macaulay

Then out spake brave Horatius,
The Captain of the Gate:
'To every man upon this earth
Death cometh soon or late.

And how can man die better
Than facing fearful odds,
For the ashes of his fathers,
And the temples of his gods?'

*Lays of Ancient Rome*

With weeping and with laughter
Still is the story told,
How well Horatius kept the bridge
In the brave days of old.

*Lays of Ancient Rome*

The Puritan hated bear-baiting, not because it gave pain
to the bear, but because it gave pleasure to the spectators.

*History of England*

There were gentlemen and there were seamen in the navy
of Charles the Second. But the seamen were not gentlemen; and the gentlemen were not seamen.

*History of England*

I shall not be satisfied unless I produce something which
shall for a few days supersede the last fashionable novel
on the tables of young ladies.

*Trevelyn's 'Life and Letters of
Macaulay'*

Thomas Babington Macaulay (1800 – 59) British historian, essayist, poet and politician, was born in Leicester
and educated at Cambridge. In 1826 he was called to the
Bar. In 1825 he published in the *Edinburgh Review* his
essay on Milton, and this was followed in the next twenty
years by numerous historical and critical essays. Macaulay
entered Parliament as a Whig (Liberal) in 1830 and advo-
cated parliamentary reform and the abolition of slavery. He
also spent several years in India as a member of the Supreme
Council, and was mainly responsible for the Indian penal
code.

# Christopher Marlowe

Was this the face that launch'd a thousand ships,
And burnt the topless towers of Ilium?

*Faustus*

O thou art fairer than the evening air,
Clad in the beauty of a thousand stars.

*Faustus*

Come live with me, and be my love,
And we will all the pleasures prove,
That valleys, groves, hills and fields,
Woods or steepy mountain yields.

*The Passionate Shepherd to*
*his Love*

Christopher Marlowe (1564–93), born in Canterbury, the son of a shoemaker, was educated at Cambridge and obtained a degree. From there he went to London, where he associated with Shakespeare and other writers of the time. Soon he attached himself to the Earl of Nottingham's theatrical company, which produced most of his plays. It has been suggested that Christopher Marlowe was part author of Shakespeare's *Titus Andronicus* and that he also wrote parts of *Henry VI* and *Edward III*.

# Groucho Marx

Saddest movie I've ever seen – I cried all the way through. Its sad when you're 82.

*On 'Last Tango in Paris'*

Groucho (Julius) Marx (1895–1977) was one of the four Marx Brothers, a team of American film comedians who started the Zeppo-Marx Agency in 1935 and appeared only in earlier films. They were known as Groucho (Julius), Harpo (Arthur), Chico (Leonard) and Zeppo (Herbert).

# John Masefield

I must go down to the seas again, to the lonely sea and the sky,
And all I ask is a tall ship and a star to steer her by –

*Sea Fever*

And the wheel's kick and the wind's song and the white
sail's shaking,
And a grey mist on the sea's face, and a grey dawn
breaking.

Sea Fever

And all I ask is a merry yarn from a laughing fellow-
rover,
And quiet sleep and a sweet dream when the long trek's
over.

Sea Fever

John Masefield (1878–1967) was born in Ledbury, Herefordshire, ran away to sea, and while in the USA worked
as a barman in New York. He returned to England and
worked on the *Manchester Guardian*, then settled in
London and attracted notice for some volumes of poetry.
Fame came with his verse narrative *The Everlasting
Mercy*, and he was later appointed poet laureate. He was
awarded the OM in 1935.

## George du Maurier

I have no talent for making new friends, but oh, such a
genius for fidelity to old ones.

Peter Ibbetson

A little work, a little play
To keep us going – and so, good-day!

A little warmth, a little light,
Of love's bestowing – and so good-night!

A little fun, to match the sorrow
Of each day's growing – and so, good-morrow!

A little trust that when we die
We reap our sowing! and so – goodbye!

Trilby

George Louis Palmella Busson Du Maurier (1834–96)
was born in Paris. His grandparents were French re-
fugees domiciled in England during the French Revolution. At the age of seventeen he went to London and
studied chemistry at University College. Later he became

an art student in Paris. After further studies in Antwerp and Dusseldorf he returned to England, and contributed illustrations to many publications. In 1865 George Du Maurier joined the staff of *Punch* and for years his pictorial satires of social life were a feature of its pages.

## André Maurois

The difficult part of an argument is not to defend one's opinion but rather to know it.

André Maurois (1885–1967) was the pseudonym of the French author Emile Herzog. In the First World War he was attached to the British Army, and his essays *Les Silences du Colonel Bramble* (1918) give humorously sympathetic observations on the British character.

## Yehudi Menuhin

The price of freedom for all musicians, both composers and interpreters, is tremendous control, discipline and patience: but perhaps not only for musicians. Do we not all find freedom to improvise, in all art, in all life, along the guiding lines of discipline?

*Theme and Variations*

Above other arts, music can be possessed without knowledge. Being an expression largely of the subconscious, it has its direct routes from whatever is in our guts, minds and spirits, without need of a detour through the classroom.

*Unfinished Journey*

Yehudi Menuhin (1916–) is an American violinist. Born of Russian-Jewish parentage, he gave his first concert at the age of eight. Two years later he made a tour of Europe, dazzling the critics by his maturity and freshness of approach. Retiring for a period of intensive study, he then achieved such a depth of interpretation, particularly in the Elgar and Beethoven concertos, that he soon became known as one of the world's greatest players. In 1963 he founded the Yehudi Menuhin School at Stoke D'Abernon, Surrey, a boarding school for talented musicians, which is the only one of its kind outside Russia.

## George Meredith

I expect that Woman will be the last thing civilised by man.

*The Ordeal of Richard
Feverel*

I've studied men from my topsy-turvey
Close, and, I reckon, rather true.
Some are fine fellows: some, right scurvy:
Most a dash between the two.

*Juggling Jerry*

She is steadfast as a star,
And yet the maddest maiden:
She can wage a gallant war,
And give the peace of Eden.

*Marian*

Lovely are the curves of the white owl sweeping,
Wavy in the dusk lit by one large star.

*Love in the Valley*

George Meredith (1828 – 1909) was a British novelist and poet. Born in Portsmouth, he was educated in Germany and then articled to a London solicitor but he soon entered journalism. He published *Poems* and *The Shaving of Shagpat* but his first realistic psychological novel, *The Ordeal of Richard Feverel*, was followed by a number of others including *The Egoist*, *Diana of the Crossways* and *The Amazing Marriage*. Later he wrote *Modern Love* and *Poems and Lyrics*.

## Alice Meynell

Thou art like silence unperplexed,
A secret and a mystery
Between one footfall and the next.

*To The Beloved*

Flocks of the memories of the day draw near
The dovecot doors of sleep.

*At Night*

Alice Christiana Gertrude Meynell (1847–1922) was a British poet and essayist whose essays include *Rhythm of Life* and *Second Person Singular*. Her youngest son, Sir Francis Meynell, founded the Nonsuch Press and was knighted in 1946.

## Michelangelo

The hand that follows intellect can achieve.

Michelangelo Buonarroti (1475–1564) was an Italian painter, sculptor, architect and poet. His early works express the humanistic ideals of the High Renaissance, but his later work shows the instability of Church and State after the Reformation and the Sack of Rome. Michelangelo's first patron was Lorenzo de Medici, and he worked for the Medici family for much of his life. Pope Julius II commissioned him to carve his tomb, but interrupted the work by telling him to paint the ceiling of the Sistine Chapel.

## George Mikes

You can keep a dog; but it is the cat who keeps people, because cats find humans useful domestic animals. A dog will flatter you but you have to flatter a cat. A dog is an employee; the cat is a freelance.

*How to be Decadent*

George Mikes (1912–) was born in Budapest and has been President of PEN in exile for many years. He has also been theatrical critic on Budapest newspapers and London correspondent of Budapest newspapers for some time. He has published a number of humorous books including *How to be an Alien, How to Scrape Skies, Wisdom for Others, Milk and Honey, Down with Everybody* and *Shakespeare and Myself*.

## John Milton

The mind is its own place, and in itself
Can make a Heav'n of Hell, a Hell of Heav'n.

*Paradise Lost*

Thus with the year
Seasons return, but not to me returns
Day or the sweet approach of ev'n or morn,
Or sight of vernal bloom, or summer's rose,
Or flocks, or herds, or human face divine;
But cloud instead, and ever-during dark
Surrounds me, from the cheerful ways of men.

*Paradise Lost*


When I consider how my light is spent,
E're half my days, in this dark world and wide,
And that one Talent which is death to hide
Lodg'd with me useless, though my Soul more bent
To serve therewith my Maker, and present
My true account.

*Sonnet On his Blindness*


I know each lane, and every alley green,
Dingle, or bushy dell, of this wild wood.
And every bosky bourn from side to side,
My daily walks and ancient neighbourhood.

*Comus*


He that has light within his own clear breast
May sit i' th' centre and enjoy bright day;
But he that hides a dark soul and foul thoughts
Benighted walks under the midday sun;
Himself is his own dungeon.

*Comus*


Fame is the spur that the clear spirit doth raise
(That last infirmity of noble mind)
To scorn delights, and live laborious days.

*Lycidas*


Haste thee, Nymph, and bring with thee
Jest and youthful jollity,
Quips and cranks, and wanton wiles,
Nods, and becks, and wreathed smiles.

*L'Allegro*

Sport that wrinkled Care derides,
And Laughter holding both his sides.
Come and trip it as ye go
On the light fantastic toe.

*L'Allegro*

The cock with lively din
Scatters the rear of darkness thin,
And to the stack, or the barn-door,
Stoutly struts his dames before...

Right against the eastern gate
Where the great sun begins his state...

Meadows trim with daisies pied,
Shallow brooks and rivers wide;
Towers and battlements it sees
Bosom'd high in tufted trees...

Towered cities please us then,
And the busy hum of men...

And pomp, and feast, and revelry,
With mask, and antique pageantry,
Such sights as youthful poets dream
On summer eves by haunted stream...

*L'Allegro*

John Milton (1604–74), son of a scrivener and composer
of music, was educated at St Paul's School and Christ's
College, Cambridge. He became a BA in 1629 and an MA
in 1632. After leaving Cambridge he lived with his father
at Horton in Buckinghamshire, and whilst there he read
the classics and prepared himself for his vocation as
a poet. After the execution of Charles 1, he published
*Tenure of Kings and Magistrates*, and was then appointed
Latin secretary to the newly-formed Council of State. He
became blind but retained his post as Latin secretary
until the Restoration, when he was arrested and fined.
He was soon released, but lost the greater part of his
fortune.

## James Monroe

A little flattery will support a man through great fatigue.

James Monroe (1758 – 1831) was fifth President of the USA. Born in Virginia he served in the War of Independence, was Minister to France from 1794 to 1796, and during 1803 negotiated the Louisiana Purchase. He was Secretary of State from 1811–15, and was elected President in 1816 and again in 1820. His name is associated with the Monroe Doctrine expressed in his message to Congress in 1823.

## Montaigne

When I play with my cat, who knows if I am more of a pastime to her than she is to me?

There is no torture that a woman would not endure to enhance her beauty.

The greatest thing in the world is to know how to be sufficient unto oneself.

The strength of any plan depends on timing.

We are all made up of fragments, so shapelessly and strangely assembled that every moment, every piece plays its own game. There is as much difference between us and ourselves as between us and others.

A learned man is not learned in all things; but an able man is able in all, even in ignorance.

No man is exempt from saying silly things. The misfortune is to say them seriously.

Dying is the greatest task we have to do, but practice can give us no assistance.

Michel Eyquem de Montaigne (1533–92), the French essayist, was born at the Château de Montaigne near Bordeaux. He studied law and became a councillor of

Bordeaux. For a time he frequented the Court of Francis II but eventually retired to his estates and wrote several volumes of *Essays* revealing his insatiable intellectual curiosity. He became preoccupied with the subject of death after the premature death of his friend La Boétie.

## Montesquieu

Civility costs nothing and buys everything.

Charles Louis de Secondat Montesquieu (1689–1755) was a French philosophical historian. Born near Bordeaux, he became adviser to the Bordeaux government in 1714 but, after the success of his *Lettres persanes* in 1721, he adopted a literary career.

## William Morris

Forget six counties overhung with smoke,
Forget the snorting steam and piston stroke,
Forget the spreading of the hideous town;
Think rather of the pack-horse on the down,
And dream of London small and white and clean,
The clear Thames bordered by its gardens green.
*Prologue to Earthly Paradise*

William Morris (1834–96), the British poet and craftsman, was born at Walthamstow and was educated at Marlborough School and Exeter College, Oxford, where he formed a lasting friendship with Edward Burne-Jones the painter and designer and was influenced by Ruskin and Rossetti. *The Earthly Paradise* was written in 1868–70, but a visit to Iceland in 1871 inspired his greatest poem *Sigurd the Volsung* and his translations of the Sagas.

## Ogden Nash

One man's remorse is another's reminiscence.

I kind of like the playful porpoise,
A healthy mind in a healthy corpus.
He and his cousin, the playful dolphin,
Why, they like swimmin' like I like golphin.

The ant has made himself illustrious
Through constant industry industrious.

The trouble with a kitten is that
Eventually it becomes a CAT.

Tell me, O Octopus, I begs,
Is those things arms, or is they legs?

Candy
Is dandy,
But liquor
Is quicker.

*Reflections on Ice-breaking*

The panther is like a leopard,
Except it hasn't been peppered.
Should you behold a panther crouch,
Prepare to say Ouch.
Better yet, if called by a panther,
Don't anther.

The truth I do not stretch or shove
When I state the dog is full of love.
I've also proved, by actual test
A wet dog is the lovingest.

*Everyone But Thee and Me,*
*The Dog*

If you should happen after dark
To find yourself in Central Park,
Ignore the paths that beckon you
And hurry, hurry to the zoo.
And creep into the tiger's lair.
Frankly, you'll be safer there.

*Everyone But Thee and Me,*
*City Greenery*

Ogden Nash (1902–71) was born in Rye, New York.
This American poet published numerous volumes of
humorous verse of impeccable technique and quietly
puncturing satire.

84

# Horatio Nelson

I have only one eye – I have a right to be blind some-times.

*At the Battle of Copenhagen,
Southey's 'Life of Nelson'*

Before this time tomorrow I shall have gained a peerage, or Westminster Abbey.

*Battle of the Nile, Southey's
'Life of Nelson'*

Horatio, Viscount Nelson (1758 – 1805) was born at Burnham Thorpe, Norfolk, and entered the navy in 1770. He saw continuous service until 1787, but returned to the navy in 1793 and fought in the Mediterranean. While commanding the Naval Brigade at Calvi, Corsica, he lost his right eye, but as Commodore in the Mediterranean he was responsible for the victory off Cape St Vincent in 1797. He lost his right arm in an engagement at Santa Cruz, and won an overwhelming victory over the French in Aboukir Bay. In 1801 he won another victory at Copenhagen, and in October 1805, now a Viscount and Commander-in-Chief, he sailed to his last victory, the Battle of Trafalgar.

# Sir Henry John Newbolt

Take my drum to England, hang et by the shore,
Strike et when your powder's runnin' low –

*The Island Race: Drake's
Drum*

There's a breathless hush in the Close to-night –
Ten to make and the match to win–
A bumping pitch and a blinding light,
An hour to play and the last man in.

*The Island Race: Vitaï
Lampada*

Sir Henry John Newbolt (1862–1938) was a British poet and also a barrister, but he was an authority on naval matters and wrote *The Year of Trafalgar* (1905) and *A Naval History of the War, 1914–18* (1920). His *Songs of the Sea* and *Songs of the Fleet* were set to music by Sir Charles Villiers Stanford, the Irish composer.

## Sir Isaac Newton

I do not know what I may appear to the world, but to myself I seem to have been only like a boy playing on the sea-shore.

*Brewsters' Memoirs of*
*Newton*

Sir Isaac Newton (1642–1727), the British philosopher, was educated at Grantham Grammar School and Trinity College, Cambridge. He discovered the binominal theorem and the differential and integral calculus and began to investigate the phenomena of universal gravitation. Soon he published his *New Theory about Light and Colours*. Later he published (with Halley) his greatest work *Philosophiae Naturalis Principia Mathematica* (1687).

## Beverley Nichols

Why this passion for shaking people out of ruts? I am devoted to ruts. Moreover, most of the people who are in ruts are much nicer, and much happier, than the people who are not. Ruts are the wise old wrinkles that civilization has traced on the earth's ancient face.

*The Gift of a Home*

Beverley Nichols (1901–83) was a writer, educated at Marlborough College and Balliol College, Oxford. For a time he was President of the Oxford Union and Editor of *Isis* and he was also founder and editor of the Oxford *Outlook*. Amongst other works he published his autobiography, *Twenty-Five*, in 1926.

## Richard Nixon

Let no one expect to make his fortune – or his reputation – by selling America short.

*22.8.1971*

There can be no whitewash at the White House.

*30.12.1973*

I let down my friends. I let down my country. I let down our system of government.

*8.5.1977*

Richard Milhous Nixon (1913–) became Republican President of the United States for two terms of office (1969–74) and during that time he negotiated the withdrawal of American troops from South Vietnam and began a process of reconciliation with China and détente with the Soviet Union. At home the Watergate scandal brought disgrace and an end to his presidency.

## Denis Norden

Middle age is when, wherever you go on holiday, you pack a sweater.

Denis Norden (1922–) is a British writer and comedian, educated at Craven Park School. He served in the RAF from 1942–45 and afterwards became staff writer in a variety agency. He first teamed up with Frank Muir in 1947, and is a very experienced and successful radio and television broadcaster.

## Kathleen Norris

From birth to eighteen a girl needs good parents. From eighteen to thirty-five she needs good looks. From thirty-five to fifty-five a woman needs personality; and from fifty-five on the old lady needs cash.

Kathleen Norris (1880–1966) was born in San Francisco, California, and spent her early years in Mill Valley, a small mountain-village in California. She was the daughter of James Alden Thompson and Josephine Moroney and married Charles Gilman Norris who died in 1945. Kathleen became librarian, social worker and writer, producing many novels. Her last one was *Family Gathering*, published in 1959.

## Alfred Noyes

The wind was a torrent of darkness among the gusty trees,
The moon was a ghostly galleon tossed upon cloudy seas,
The road was a ribbon of moonlight over the purple moor,
And the highwayman came riding –
The highwayman came riding, up to the old inn door.
*The Highwayman*

Go down to Kew in lilac-time (it isn't far from London)
And you shall wander hand in hand with love in summer's wonderland.

*The Barrel Organ*

Alfred Noyes (1880–1958) was a British poet who was
educated at Oxford and later became professor of modern
English literature at Princeton University. His best-
known poems include *The Highwayman* and *The Barrel
Organ*, but he also wrote *Drake*, *The Torch Bearers* and
*The Accusing Ghost*, which was an attempt to clear the
name of Roger Casement.


## Omar Khayyam

Awake! for Morning in the Bowl of Night
Has flung the Stone that puts the Stars to Flight
And Lo! the Hunter of the East has caught
The Sultan's Turret in a Noose of Light.

*Rubaiyat*

Here with a Loaf of Bread beneath the bough,
A Flask of Wine, A Book of Verse – and Thou
Beside me singing in the Wilderness –
And Wilderness is Paradise enow.

*Rubaiyat*

'Tis all a Chequer-board of Nights and Days
Where Destiny with Men for Pieces plays:
Hither and thither moves, and mates, and slays,
And one by one back in the Closet Lays.

*Rubaiyat*

The Moving Finger writes: and, having writ,
Moves on: nor all thy Piety nor Wit
Shall lure it back to cancel half a Line,
Nor all thy Tears wash out a Word of it.

*Rubaiyat*

Think, in this batter'd Caravanserai
Whose Doorways are alternate Night and Day,
How Sultan after Sultan with his Pomp
Abode his Hour or two, and went his way.

*Rubaiyat*

Ah, make the most of what we yet may spend,
Before we too into Dust descend;
Dust into Dust, and under Dust, to lie,
Sans Wine, sans Song, sans Singer, and – sans End!

*Rubaiyat*

Ah, Moon of my Delight who know'st no wane,
The Moon of Heav'n is rising once again:
How oft hereafter rising shall she look
Through this same Garden, after me – in vain!

*Rubaiyat*

Omar Khayyam was an eleventh-century astronomer and
poet whose name 'Khayyam' means 'tent-maker'. He was
born at Naishapur in Khorassan in the latter half of the
century. The stanzas contain the poet's meditations on
the mysteries of existence, and his counsel to drink and
make merry while life lasts. His work was translated into
the English poetic version by Edward FitzGerald.

# Ovid

Take rest; a field that has rested gives a beautiful crop.

Ovid (43BC–AD17) was a Roman poet, whose full name
was Publius Ovidius Naso. He was born at Sulmo and
studied rhetoric in Rome in preparation for a legal career
but soon turned to literature. In AD8 he was banished by
Augustus to Tomi on the Black Sea, where he died. This
punishment was supposedly for his immoral *Ars Amatoria* but was probably due to some connection with Julia,
the profligate daughter of Augustus.

# John Owen

God and the doctor we alike adore
But only when in danger, not before;
The danger o'er, both are alike requited,
God is forgotten, and the doctor slighted.

*Epigrams*

Times change, and we change with them too.

*Epigrams*

John Owen (1560?–1622), the Welsh epigrammatist, was a master of Latin idioms and the author of a number of shrewd and pointed epigrams.

## Robert Owen

All the world is queer save thee and me, and even thou art a little queer.

> *On separating from his*
> *business partner, William*
> *Allen, in 1828*

Robert Owen (1771–1858) became a British socialist and co-operator, and manager of a mill at New Lanark where, by improving working and housing conditions and by providing schools, he created a model community. Later he organised the Grand National Consolidated Trades Union, and his ideas did much to stimulate the co-operative movement.

## Ignacz Jean Paderewski

Piano playing is more difficult than statesmanship. It is harder to awake emotions in ivory keys than it is in human beings.

Ignacz Jean Paderewski (1860–1941) was a Polish pianist, composer and statesman. The son of a Polish patriot, he gained European and American fame after his debut in Vienna in 1887 and became a noted exponent of Chopin. During the First World War he raised money in America for the relief of Polish war victims and organised the Polish army in France. In 1919 as Prime Minister he represented the newly independent Poland at the Peace Conference.

## Thomas Paine

The sublime and the ridiculous are often so nearly related, that it is difficult to class them separately. One step above the sublime makes the ridiculous, and one step above the ridiculous makes the sublime again.

> *The Age of Reason*

Thomas Paine (1737–1809) was born in Thetford, but he went to America and there published *Common Sense* which was an influential republican pamphlet. He fought for the colonists in the War of Independence. In 1787 he returned to England and soon published *The Rights of Man*, which was an answer to Burke's *Reflections on the Revolution in France*, but in 1792 he was indicted for treason. He escaped to France, where he represented Calais in the Convention but, after narrowly escaping the guillotine, he regained his seat after the fall of Robespierre. In 1793 he published *The Age of Reason*, and eventually returned to America, where he died.

## Dorothy Parker

Guns aren't lawful,
Nooses give:
Gas smells awful:
You might as well live.

*Résumé*

Down from Caesar past Joynson-Hicks
Echoes the warning, ever new;
Though they're trained to amusing tricks,
Gentler, they, than the pigeon's coo,
Careful, son, of the cursed two –
Either one is a dangerous pet;
Natural history proves it true –
Women and elephants never forget.

*Ballade of Unfortunate Mammals*

Congratulations: we all knew you had it in you.

*Telegram to a friend who had
just had a baby*

She ran the whole gamut of her emotions, from A to B.

*Remark about an actress*

Byron and Shelley and Keats
Were a trio of lyrical treats.
The forehead of Shelley was cluttered with curls,
And Keats never was a descendant of earls,
And Byron walked out with a number of girls...

*The Lives and Times of
Keats, Shelley and Byron*

Four be the things I'd be better without,
Love, curiosity, freckles, and doubt.

*Inventory*

O, is it then, Utopian
To hope that I may meet a man
Who'll not relate, in accents suave,
The tales of girls he used to have?

*De Profundis*

That woman speaks eighteen languages, and she can't say
'no' in any of them.

Dorothy Parker (1893–1967) was an American writer,
born in the West End of New Jersey into the famous
Rothschild family. She became Mrs Alan Campbell, and
wrote verse and a number of short stories, quickly
establishing a reputation for an acid wit and scathing
comment.

## Blaise Pascal

The heart has its reasons which reason knows nothing of.

Imagination is the deceitful part of man, a mistress of
error and falsity who cheats us the more because she does
not cheat us always.

If you want people to think well of you, do not speak well
of yourself.

Can anything be more ridiculous than that a man should
have the right to kill me because he lives on the other side
of the water and because his ruler has a quarrel with
mine?

Blaise Pascal (1632–62), the French philosopher and
mathematician, was a precocious student. He investi-
gated the laws governing the weight of air, the equilib-
rium of liquids, the hydraulic press, the infinitesimal
calculus, and the mathematical theory of probability.

## James Payn

I had never had a piece of toast
Particularly long and wide,
But fell upon the sanded floor
And always on the buttered side.

*Chambers's Journal*

James Payn (1830–98), the English novelist, was editor of *Chambers's Journal* from 1859 to 1874, and of *The Cornhill Magazine* from 1883 to 1896. He was also author of a number of novels including *Lost Sir Massingberd*.

## Samuel Pepys

This morning came home my fine camlet cloak, with gold buttons, and a silk suit, which cost me much money, and I pray God to make me able to pay for it.

*Diary, 1 July 1660*

I went out to Charing Cross, to see Major-general Harrison hanged, drawn and quartered; which was done there, he looking as cheerful as any man could do in that condition.

*Diary, 13 Oct 1660*

My wife, who, poor wretch, is troubled with her lonely life.

*Diary, 19 Dec 1662*

Went to hear Mrs Turner's daughter ... play on the harpsichon; but, Lord! it was enough to make any man sick to hear her; yet was I forced to commend her highly.

*Diary, 1 May 1663*

Saw a wedding in the church ... and strange to say what delight we married people have to see these poor fools decoyed into our condition.

*Diary, 25 Dec 1665*

Home, and, being washing-day, dined upon cold meat.

*Diary, 4 April 1666*

To church; and with my mourning, very handsome, and new periwig, make a great show.

*Diary, 31 March 1667*

Samuel Pepys (1633–1703) the British diarist, was born in London. He entered the navy office in 1660, shortly after beginning his diary. Appointed secretary to the Admiralty in 1672, he was later imprisoned, with loss of office, on suspicion of being connected with the Popish Plot. Reinstated in 1684 but finally deprived at the 1688 Revolution, he retired to Clapham. Pepys' *Diary* was written in his own personal version of Shelton's short-hand, and was not deciphered until 1825. Discontinued in 1669 because of his failing sight, it is nevertheless unrivalled for its intimacy and the graphic picture it gives of seventeenth-century English life.

## Johann Heinrich Pestalozzi

To change people you must love them. Your influence reaches only as far as your love.

Johann Heinrich Pestalozzi (1746–1827), born at Zurich, was a Swiss educationalist. He established an experimental school at Burgdorf in 1799, and moved it to Yverdon in 1805.

## Pablo Picasso

I do not seek – I find.

Pablo Ruiz Picasso (1881–1973) was a famous Spanish artist, son of art teacher José Ruiz Blasco and an Andalusian mother Maria Picasso Lopez, but he discontinued the use of the name Ruiz in 1898. Born at Malaga, he was a mature artist at ten, and at sixteen was holding his first exhibition. From 1901–4 he had his Blue Period, when he painted mystic distorted figures in blue tones, and followed this with his Rose Period, Cubism, etc. He was unique in the fertile vigour of his invention, and his exhibitions attracted a large popular following.

## William Pitt

Confidence is a plant of slow growth in an aged bosom; youth the season of credulity.

*Speech in House of Commons,*
*14.1.1766*

The poorest man may in his cottage bid defiance to all the forces of the crown. It may be frail – its roof may shake – the wind may blow through it – the storm may enter – but the King of England may not enter ...

*Speech on the Excise Bill*

William Pitt (1708–78), first Earl of Chatham, entered Parliament as MP for Old Sarum and gained a reputation for himself by his attacks on the Prime Minister, Sir Robert Walpole. For a time he was Paymaster-General. He helped to form the ministry which continued the war against the French (Seven Years' War), and was largely responsible for the British victories in Canada and India and on the seas.

# Plato

Philosophy is a longing after heavenly wisdom.

Pleasure is the greatest incentive to evil.

Self-conquest is the greatest of victories.

Plato (c429–347BC) the Greek philosopher, was born in Athens. He had political ambitions but came under the influence of Socrates and about the year 387BC founded the Academy of Athens, an institute for the study of philosophy. Plato remained in Athens except for two visits to Syracuse in 367 and 361–60BC.

# Plutarch

I don't need a friend who changes when I change and who nods when I nod; my shadow does that much better.

Plutarch (AD46–120) was born in Greece at Chacronea, lectured on philosophy at Rome and was appointed procurator of Greece by Hadrian. His *Parallel Lives* consists of pairs of biographies of Greek and Roman soldiers and statesmen, followed by comparisons between the two. North's translation inspired Shakespeare's Roman plays.

## Edgar Allan Poe

Helen, thy beauty is to me
Like those Nicaean barks of yore,
That gently, o'er a perfumed sea,
The weary, wayworn, wanderer bore
To his own native shore.

On desperate seas long wont to roam
Thy hyacinth hair, thy classic face,
Thy Naiad airs, have brought me home
To the glory that was Greece
And the grandeur that was Rome.

*To Helen*

Edgar Allan Poe (1809–49) was an American author born
in Boston but orphaned at the age of two. He was
brought up by a Mr and Mrs Allan, whose surname he
used as a middle name from 1824. After a period of
poverty and alcoholism and the death of his wife, he
concentrated on writing poems of melancholy beauty.
His reputation rests on short stories of horrific atmosphere such as *The Fall of the House of Usher*, and certain
detective stories such as *The Gold Bug* and *The Murders in
the Rue Morgue* which laid the foundations of modern
detective fiction.

## Alexander Pope

Happy the man whose wish and care
A few paternal acres bound,
Content to breathe his native air,
In his own ground.

*Ode on Solitude*

Words are like leaves; and where they most abound,
Much fruit of sense beneath is rarely found.

*An Essay on Criticism*

Be not the first by whom the new are tried,
Nor yet the last to lay the old aside.

*An Essay on Criticism*

To err is human, to forgive, divine.

*An Essay on Criticism*

Where'er you find 'the cooling western breeze',
In the next line, it 'whispers through the trees'.
If crystal streams 'with pleasing murmurs' creep,
The reader's threaten'd (not in vain) with 'sleep'.

*An Essay on Criticism*

True ease in writing comes from art, not chance,
As those move easiest who have learn'd to dance.

*An Essay on Criticism*

For fools rush in where angels fear to tread.

*An Essay on Criticism*

Hope springs eternal in the human breast;
Man never is, but always to be blest.

*An Essay on Man*

'Yet Chloe sure was formed without a spot'
Nature in her then erred not, but forgot.
'With every pleasing, every prudent part,
Say, what can Chloe want? – She wants a heart.'

*Characters, Chloe*

Virtue may choose the high or low degree,
'Tis just alike to Virtue, and to me;
Dwell in a monk, or light upon a king,
She's still the same, beloved, contented thing.

*The Triumph of Vice*

Come, lovely nymph, and bless the silent hours,
When swains from shearing seek their nightly bowers;
When weary reapers quit the sultry field,
And, crowned with corn, their thanks to Ceres yield,
This harmless grove no lurking viper hides,
But in my breast the serpent Love abides.

*Sylvan Delights*

Alexander Pope (1688–1744) was the son of a Roman
Catholic linen-draper of London. A severe illness at the
age of twelve ruined his health and distorted his figure,
but he showed his literary skill in his *Pastorals* when he
was sixteen. He became known to Joseph Addison's
circle and soon published his *Messiah*, which was followed by his *Rape of the Lock*. His *Ode for Music on St.
Cecilia's Day* was not very successful, but he also pub-

lished *Windsor Forest* which was well received. He moved from Addison's circle and became a member of the Scriblerus Club, an association which included Swift, Gay, Arbuthnot and other famous writers.

## Richard Porson

I went to Frankfort where I got drunk
With that most learn'd professor, Brunck;
I went to Worms, and got more drunken
With that more learn'd professor, Ruhnken.

*Facetiae Cantabrigienses,*
*1825*

Richard Porson (1759–1808), a Regius professor of Greek at Cambridge, edited four plays of Euripides. His finest single piece of criticism was his supplement to the preface to his *Hecuba*. His elucidation of Greek idiom and usage and his editing of texts advanced Greek scholarship.

## Dilys Powell

Society splits into cat-lovers and dog-lovers. For years I cared chiefly for cats. Later I came round to dogs as well – to dogs, I mean, as sharers of bed and board. A cat is a house guest. A dog joins the family. He makes friends for you, or at any rate, acquaintances. People one might never have spoken to greet one warmly; they know your dog's name when you remain anonymous.

*Animals in My Life*
*Sunday Times, 27 June 1976*

Dilys Powell CBE (1901–) was *Sunday Times* film critic from 1939–76 and now reviews films for *Punch*. She is the author of several books, including *The Villa Ariadne*.

## Enoch Powell

A little nonsense now and then is not a bad thing. Where would we politicians be if we were not allowed to talk it sometimes?

*On Politics, 19.12.1965*

History is littered with wars which everybody knew would never happen.

*On War, 22.10.1967*

As I look ahead I am filled with foreboding. Like the Roman, I seem to see 'The River Tiber' foaming with much blood.

*Speech at Birmingham, April 1968,*<br>*a reference to Virgil's 'Aeneid'*

You don't lead people by following them, but by saying what they want to follow.

*6.12.1970*

All political lives, unless they are cut off in mid-stream at a happy juncture, end in failure, because that is the nature of politics and of human affairs.

John Enoch Powell (1912–) was educated at King Edward's School, Birmingham, and Trinity College, Cambridge. He became Craven Travelling Student of 1933, Fellow of Trinity College, Cambridge, from 1934–8, and Professor of Greek in the University of Sydney, Australia, from 1937–9. He has been MP for South Down since 1974. Often an outspoken and controversial figure, Enoch Powell has held various appointments on the British General Staff, has been Parliamentary Secretary of the Ministry of Housing and Local Government, Financial Secretary to the Treasury, and Minister of Health.

## J.B. Priestley

Fountains enchant me – in the daytime, when the sunlight turns their scattered drops into diamonds; after dark when coloured lights are played on them, and the night rains emeralds, rubies, sapphires.

*Essays*

As a rule I like local accents, and have kept one myself. They make for a variety in speech and they give men's talk a flavour of the particular countryside to which at heart they belong. Standard English is like standard anything else – poor tasteless stuff.

*English Journey*

To travel swiftly in a closed car, as so many of us do nowadays, is to cut oneself off from the reality of the regions one passes through, perhaps from any sane reality at all. Whole leagues of countryside are only a roar and a muddle outside the windows, and villages are only like brick-coloured bubbles that we burst as we pass. Their life is temporarily as remote as the moon.

*English Journey*

John Boynton Priestly (1894 –), the prolific British novelist, was born in Bradford, the son of a schoolmaster. He was educated at Trinity Hall, Cambridge, and served in the First World War. He established his reputation as a novelist with *The Good Companions* and later wrote *Angel Pavement, Dangerous Corner, An Inspector Calls*, and other well-known plays.

## HRH Prince Philip

It is no good shutting your eyes and saying 'British is Best' three times a day after meals, and expecting it to be so.

*29 April 1956*

I have been wet and frozen, and fried in the sun. I have walked for miles through fields and over hills; I have frightened myself silly climbing to the top of rickety pigeon platforms, and I have sat shivering on the edge of a kale field in a blizzard.

To anyone with a conventional view of pleasure, to the town-living, comfort-loving commuter, the idea that there might be any thrill in wildfowling or rough shooting must seem too painfully ludicrous to be considered...

...Yet this is the stuff of natural history, this is a certain way to arouse enthusiasm for conservation. Without this introduction I would never have learnt about the sights and sounds of the country and the wilderness.

*Published in Saturday*
*Evening Post*

HRH Prince Philip, Duke of Edinburgh (1921–) is a grandson of George I of Greece and a great-grandson of Queen Victoria. He was born in Corfu but raised in England and educated at Gordonstoun and Dartmouth Naval College. A naturalised British subject taking the surname of Mountbatten in March 1947, he married Princess Elizabeth (later Queen Elizabeth II) in Westminster Abbey, having the previous day received the title Duke of Edinburgh. In 1956 he founded the Duke of Edinburgh's Award Scheme to encourage creative achievement among young people.

## Matthew Prior

Be to her virtues very kind;
Be to her faults a little blind;
Let all her ways be unconfin'd;
And clap your padlock – on her mind.

*An English Padlock*

For, as our different ages move,
'Tis so ordain'd (would Fate but mind it!)
That I shall be past making love
When she begins to comprehend it.

*To a Child of Quality Five
Years Old (The author then
forty)*

Dear Chloe, how blubbered is that pretty face!
Thy cheek all on fire, and thy hair all uncurled.
Prithee, quit this caprice; and (as old Falstaff says)
Let us e'en talk a little like folks of this world.

How cans't thou presume thou hast leave to destroy
The beauties which Venus but lent to thy keeping?
Those looks were designed to inspire love and joy:
More ordinary eyes may serve people for weeping…

What I speak, my fair Chloe, and what I write, shows
The difference there is betwixt Nature and Art:
I court others in verse, but I love thee in prose;
And they have my whimsies, but thou hast my heart.

*Answer to Chloe Jealous*

Matthew Prior (1664–1721) was born in Dorset, the son of a joiner, and educated at Westminster School (under the patronage of Lord Dorset) and St John's College, Cambridge. He entered the diplomatic service in 1691, was appointed secretary to the ambassador at the Hague and employed in the negotiations for the Treaty of Ryswick. In 1697 this treaty ended the war between Great Britain, Austria, Spain and their allies on one side and France on the other. He joined the Tories and in 1711 was sent to Paris as a secret agent at the time of peace negotiations. The War of the Spanish Succession culminated in the Treaty of Utrecht (1713), popularly known as 'Matt's Peace'. On Queen Anne's death in 1714 he was imprisoned for two years. After his release a folio edition of his poems was brought out by his admirers, by which he gained the sum of four thousand guineas.

## Francis Quarles

Even like two little bank-dividing brooks,
That wash the pebbles with their wanton streams,
And having ranged and searched a thousand nooks,
Meet both at length in silver-breasted Thames
Where in a greater current they conjoin:
So I my Best-Beloved's am, so he is mine.

Even so we met; and after long pursuit
Even so we joined; we both became entire;
No need for either to renew a suit,
For I was flax and he was flames of fire:
Our firm united souls did more than twine,
So I my Best-Beloved's am, so he is mine.

He gives me wealth, I give him all my vows;
I give him songs, he gives me length of days;
With wreaths of grace he crowns my conquering brows;
And I his temples with a crown of praise...

*My Beloved is Mine and I am His*

My soul, sit thou a patient looker-on;
Judge not the play before the play is done:
Her plot has many changes; every day
Speaks a new scene; the last act crowns the play.

*Epigram*

Francis Quarles (1592–1644) was a metaphysical poet. He went abroad in the suite of Princess Elizabeth, daughter of James I, on her marriage with the Elector Palatine, and wrote pamphlets in defence of Charles I, which led to the sequestration of his property. He is chiefly remembered for his *Emblems*, a book of short devotional poems which was published in 1635.

## François Rabelais

A child is not a vase to be filled, but a fire to be lit.

François Rabelais (1494–1553) was a French author, born at Chinon, Touraine. He became a monk and, having studied medicine, lectured on anatomy. He wrote several great works, particularly some satirical allegories which were laced with coarseness, broad humour and philosophy.

## Ronald Reagan

I don't think anyone would cheerfully want to use atomic weapons – but the enemy should go to bed every night being afraid that we might.

> *Remark in July 1967, during*
> *a grim period of the Vietnam*
> *War*

All of us were expecting it to be a cliffhanger.

> *Surprised remark on*
> *being elected*
> *Republican President of USA,*
> *November 1980*

Ronald Reagan (1911–) began his career as an actor in America in the thirties, starred in fifty films, and later became well known on television. In 1967 he became Republican Governor of California. In 1968 he made a bid for the Republican presidential nomination, which was unsuccessful, but in 1980, by a landslide victory, he was elected 40th President of the USA, to succeed President Carter in that office on 20 January 1981.

## Sir Joshua Reynolds

It is allowed on all hands, that facts, and events, however they may bind the historian, have no dominion over the poet or the painter. With us, history is made to bend and conform to this grand idea of art...

These arts, in their highest province, are not addressed to the gross senses; but to the desires of the mind, to that spark of divinity which we have within.

*Discourses, The Aims of Art*

Sir Joshua Reynolds (1723–92), the British artist, was born near Plymouth. He went to London at the age of seventeen and was apprenticed to Thomas Hudson, a mediocre portrait painter. For several years he was active as a portrait painter in London and Plymouth, but in 1749 he went abroad to complete his studies. After living in Rome and other Italian cities he settled in London and became the most famous portrait painter of his day and the first President of the Royal Academy.

## Sir Ralph Richardson

We actors are the jockeys of literature. The dramatist writes the plays; we try to make them run.

Sir Ralph David Richardson (1902 – 83) was born in Cheltenham and had an extensive career on stage from 1921 and in films from 1933. He also achieved great success as actor-director of the Old Vic from 1944 to 1947.

## George Robey

I am satiated with fishing stories – there's no truth in them! The man who caught that fish is a blasted liar.

*Comment on seeing a stuffed fish in a glass case*

(Sir) George Robey (1869–1954) was the stage-name of British comedian George Edward Wade. Posing as 'The Prime Minister of Mirth' and dressed in close-buttoned frock-coat and semi-clerical bowler, he sang such songs as 'Tempt Me Not'. He was a master of significant gesture and voice inflection, and was distinguished by his bushy eyebrows.

## La Rochefoucauld

Before strongly desiring anything, we should look carefully into the happiness of its present owner.

François, Duc de la Rochefoucauld (1613–80) was born in Paris, became a soldier and took part in the wars of the Fronde. His later years were divided between the Court and literary society. He is best known for his work *Réflexions, Sentences et Maximes Morales* (1665).

## J.D. Rockefeller

It's easy to run into debt, but hard to crawl out even at a slow walk.

John Davison Rockefeller (1839–1937) organised the Standard Oil Company of America in 1870 and substituted combination for competition, becoming immensely rich in the process. From 1890 he undertook the philanthropic distribution of his fortune, and by the end of 1927 was said to have bestowed some £100,000,000 on such purposes.

## Will Rogers

It's great to be great, but it's greater to be human.

Will Rogers (1879–1935) was an American rustic comedian. For a time he was in the Ziegfeld Follies, but later became famous for many films, including *Almost a Husband*, *The Gay Caballero* and *The Strongest Man in the World*.

## Mickey Rooney

I'm learning every day. Life wouldn't be any fun if it didn't have its ups and downs.

*In an interview for 'Woman's Realm'*

It isn't how tall you are. It's what you do with yourself that counts.

*In an interview for 'Woman's Realm'*

Mickey Rooney (1920–) was a working actor from the age of fifteen months, and first appeared in Vaudeville with his parents. He later became a businessman and worked for dozens of companies. A much-married man, Mickey Rooney had had eight wives up until 1980, beating even Henry VIII's record!

## Christina Rossetti

Better by far you should forget and smile
Than that you should remember and be sad.

*Remember*

My heart is like a singing bird
Whose nest is in a watered shoot;
My heart is like an apple-tree
Whose boughs are bent with thickset fruit;
My heart is like a rainbow shell
That paddles in a halcyon sea;
My heart is gladder than all these
Because my love is come to me.

*A Birthday*

Does the road wind up-hill all the way?
Yes, to the very end.
Will the day's journey take the whole long day?
From morn to night, my friend.
But is there for the night a resting-place?
A roof for when the slow, dark hours begin...

*Uphill*

Christina Georgina Rossetti (1830–94), the British poet and sister of the poet and artist Dante Gabriel Rossetti, was a devout Anglican. She produced much popular lyric and religious verse.

## Gioachino Antonio Rossini

Give me a laundry list and I'll set it to music.

Gioachino Antonio Rossini (1792–1868) was an Italian composer. Born at Pesaro, his first success was the opera *Tancredi*, but three years later his *Il Barbiere di Siviglia* was produced at Rome. At first it was a failure. Rossini had a fertile composition period from 1815–23 during which time he produced twenty operas. After *Guillaume Tell* (1829) he gave up writing opera and spent his time in Bologna and Paris.

## Jean-Jacques Rousseau

To live is not merely to breathe, it is to act.

Man was born free, and everywhere he is in fetters.
*Du Contrat Social*

He who is slowest in making a promise is most faithful in its performance.

Jean-Jacques Rousseau (1712–78) was a French philosopher who was born in Geneva. He was apprenticed to a lawyer and engraver but ran away and for some time led the wandering life described in his *Confessions*. Later he published *A Discourse on The Origin of Inequality* which made him famous.

## John Ruskin

To see clearly is poetry, prophesy, and religion, all in one.
*Modern Painters*

I have seen, and heard, much of Cockney impudence before now; but never expected to hear a coxcomb ask two hundred guineas for flinging a pot of paint in the public's face.
*On Whistler's 'Nocturne in Black and Gold', Fors Clavigera*

John Ruskin (1819–1900) was the son of James Ruskin, a partner in a wine business. In 1843 he published anonymously the first volume of the famous *Modern Painters*, of which five volumes were issued over a period of seventeen years. This first volume, written when Ruskin was only twenty-four, was conceived in a mood of indignation at the artistic ignorance of England, and written in particular to defend Turner against the attacks on his paintings. Ruskin made the acquaintance of Turner in 1840 and of Millais in 1851.

In 1849 he published his *Seven Lamps of Architecture*, which dealt with the leading principles of architecture, but which was mainly a defence of Gothic as the noblest style. *The Stones of Venice*, a treatise in three volumes, was written while the production of *Modern Painters* was continuing and its purpose was to glorify Gothic architecture and expose 'the pestilent art of the Renaissance' by attacking it in its central stronghold, Venice itself.

# Bertrand Russell

Every man who has acquired some unusual skill enjoys exercising it until it has become a matter of course, or until he can no longer improve himself. This motive to activity begins in early childhood: a boy who can stand on his head becomes reluctant to stand on his feet.

A great deal of work gives the same pleasure that is to be derived from games of skill.

The work of a lawyer or a politician must contain in a more delectable form a great deal of the same pleasure that is to be derived from playing bridge. Here, of course, there is not only the exercise of skill but the outwitting of a skilled opponent.

A man who can do stunts in an aeroplane finds the pleasure so great that for the sake of it he is willing to risk his life.

*The Exercise of Skill from*
*'The Conquest of Happiness'*

Bertrand Arthur William Russell (1872–1970) was a British philosopher and mathematician. Born at Trelleck, the grandson of the first Earl Russell (Lord John Russell), he was educated at Trinity College, Cambridge, where he specialised in mathematics and became a lecturer. His pacifist attitude in the First World War lost him the lectureship, and he served six months in prison for an article he wrote in a pacifist journal. After the war he went to Russia, China and the USA, where he taught at many universities. Later he returned to England and wrote many books, being awarded the OM in 1949 and the Nobel Prize for literature in 1950. On the death of his brother in 1931 he succeeded to the earldom, becoming the third earl.

## George Sand

We cannot tear out a single page from our life, but we can throw the whole book into the fire.

Life is a slate where all our sins are written; from time to time we rub the sponge of repentance over it so we can begin sinning again.

George Sand (1804–76) was the pseudonym of French novelist Armandine Aurore Lucile Dupin, who married young but separated from her husband and lived in Paris as a writer. Subsequent relations with Alfred de Musset and Chopin were to influence her work.

## George Santayana

We live experimentally, moodily, in the dark; each generation breaks its eggshell with the same haste and assurance as the last, pecks at the same indigestible pebbles, dreams the same dreams, or others just as absurd, and if it hears anything of what former men have learnt by experience, it corrects their maxims by its first impressions.

England is pre-eminently a land of atmosphere. A luminous haze permeates everywhere, softening distances, magnifying perspective, transfiguring familiar objects, harmonizing the accidental, making beautiful things magical and ugly things picturesque.

Mists prolong the most sentimental and soothing of hours, the twilight, through the long summer evenings and the whole winter's day.

*Soliloquies in England*

George Santayana (1863–1952) was a Spanish philosopher. Born in Madrid, he graduated at Harvard where he taught the history of philosophy from 1889 to 1911. He wrote a number of books on philosophy, several volumes of poems and the novel *The Last Puritan*.

## Robert Schumann

In order to compose, all you need is to remember a tune that nobody else has thought of.

Robert Schumann (1810–56) was a German musician. Born at Zwickau, Saxony, he taught at Leipzig Conservatoire and was musical director at Düsseldorf from 1850 to 1853. As a composer he excelled in pianoforte compositions and in *Lieder*. His piano concerto Opus 54 and sonatas Opus 11 and 22 are particularly famous.

## Albert Schweitzer

Many women were dying in childbirth. The elders warned them never to see a doctor, that it would bring bad luck. How can I gain power over these old witches? I thought.
Then I hit on the idea of presenting each baby born at my hospital with a little bonnet and dress. By sheer bribery, my power was established, and pregnant women have flocked to the hospital ever since.

*Reader's Digest, September 1980*

Albert Schweitzer (1875–1965), the French theologian, was also an organist and missionary surgeon. He founded a hospital in 1913 at Lambarene, Republic of Gabon. He remained there apart from the brief intervals spent giving recitals of organ music, mainly Bach, in order to raise funds for his medical work. He was awarded the Nobel Peace Prize in 1952.

# Robert Falcon Scott

We are in a desperate state, feet frozen etc. No fuel and a long way from food, but it would do your heart good to be in our tent, to hear our songs and the cheery conversation.

*Farewell letter to Sir J.M. Barrie*

For God's sake look after our people.

*Journal, 25.3.1912*

Had we lived, I should have had a tale to tell of the hardihood, endurance and courage of my companions which would have stirred the heart of every Englishman.

These rough notes and our dead bodies must tell the tale.

Robert Falcon Scott (1868–1912), the British Antarctic explorer, entered the navy in 1882. Later he commanded two Antarctic expeditions, first in the *Discovery* (1901–4) and then in the *Terra Nova* (1910–12). On 18 January 1912 he reached the South Pole, only to discover that the Norwegian explorer Amundsen had already been there. On the return journey he and his companions, Wilson, Oates, Bowers, and Evans, perished. His journal was recovered and published. His son Peter is well known as a naturalist and for his paintings of birds.

# Sir Walter Scott

Like the dew on the mountain,
Like the foam on the river,
Like the bubble on the fountain,
Thou art gone, and for ever!

*The Lady of the Lake*

The way was long, the wind was cold,
The Minstrel was infirm and old;
His wither'd cheek and tresses grey,
Seem'd to have known a better day.
The harp, his sole remaining joy
Was carried by an orphan boy,
The last of all the Bards was he,
Who sung of Border chivalry.

*The Lay of the Last Minstrel*

But, my Lord, there is a Southern proverb – fine words butter no parsnips.

*Rob Roy*

Sir Walter Scott (1771 – 1832), a Scottish poet and novelist, was born in Edinburgh of gentle blood, but his early education was interrupted by delicate health, coupled with lameness. He attended High School and University, and at about 15 he entered the office of his father, a Writer to the Signet and later Sheriff of Selkirkshire and Clerk of Session. Called to the Bar in 1792, Scott's interest in the old Border tales and ballads was early awakened. He devoted much of his leisure to the exploration of the Border country, and in 1802/3 there appeared the three volumes of his *Minstrelsy of the Scottish Border*. The first of his long poems – *The Lay of the Last Minstrel* – was published in 1805 and attracted immediate and widespread attention. *Marimon, The Lady of the Lake* and *Rokeby* followed in rapid succession, and *Waverley* appeared anonymously in 1810, taking the world by storm.

Being eclipsed to a certain extent by Byron as a poet, Scott turned his attention to the novel. *Waverley* was followed by *Guy Mannering*, and a number of others including *Rob Roy, The Heart of Midlothian, Tales of my Landlord, The Bride of Lammermoor* and *A Legend of Montrose*. Scott continued to write novels, but became involved in the bankruptcy of Constable and Co and liable for a debt of £114,000. He shouldered the whole burden himself, and shortened his own life by his efforts to pay off the creditors, who all received full payment after his death.

## John Selden

Old friends are best. King James used to call for his old shoes; they were easiest for his feet.

*Table Talk: Friends*

A King is a thing men have made for their own sakes.

*Table Talk: Of a King*

John Selden (1584 –1654), an eminent lawyer and bencher of the Inner Temple, won fame as an orientalist. Reports of his utterances appeared in *Table Talk* from time to time during the last twenty years of his life and were collected by his secretary, Richard Milward.

# Seneca

Never judge your neighbour until you have been in the same situation.

Travel and change of place impart new vigour to the mind.

It is often better not to see an insult than to attempt to revenge it.

If you are surprised at the number of our maladies, count your cooks.

Lucius Annaeus Seneca (died AD65), a philosopher, was tutor to the young Nero, and when Nero became Emperor he was one of his chief advisors. He tried to check Nero's vices. Seneca's writings include works on moral philosophy and nine tragedies in a rhetorical style. He was accused of participating in the conspiracy of Piso and was ordered to take his own life, which he did with stoic courage.

# William Shakespeare

Men are April when they woo, December when they wed: maids are May when they are maids, but the sky changes when they are wives.

*As You Like It*

All the world's a stage,
And all the men and women merely players:
They have their exits and their entrances;
And one man in his time plays many parts.

*As You Like It*

For this relief much thanks; 'tis bitter cold,
And I am sick at heart.

*Hamlet*

To be or not to be: that is the question:
Whether 'tis nobler in the mind to suffer
The slings and arrows of outrageous fortune,
Or to take arms against a sea of troubles,
And by opposing end them?

*Hamlet*

Neither a borrower, nor a lender be;
For loan oft loses both itself and friend,
And borrowing dulls the edge of husbandry.

*Hamlet*


This above all: to thine own self be true,
And it must follow, as the night the day,
Thou canst not then be false to any man.

*Hamlet*


Let me have men about me that are fat;
Sleek-headed men and such as sleep o'nights:
Yond Cassius has a lean and hungry look;
He thinks too much – such men are dangerous.

*Julius Caesar*


Let's carve him as a dish fit for the gods,
Not hew him as a carcass fit for hounds.

*Julius Caesar*


Cowards die many times before their deaths;
The valiant never taste of death but once.

*Julius Caesar*


Truth will come to light; murder cannot be hid long.

*The Merchant of Venice*


The man that hath no music in himself
Nor is not moved with concord of sweet sounds,
Is fit for treasons, stratagems and spoils –

*The Merchant of Venice*


How far that little candle throws his beams!
So shines a good deed in a naughty world.

*The Merchant of Venice*


It is a wise father that knows his own child.

*The Merchant of Venice*


The devil can cite Scripture for his purpose.

*The Merchant of Venice*

O! swear not by the moon, the inconstant moon,
That monthly changes in her circled orb,
Lest that thy love prove likewise variable.

*Romeo and Juliet*

Night's candles are burnt out, and jocund day
Stands on tiptoe on the misty mountain tops.

*Romeo and Juliet*

What's in a name? That which we call a rose
By any other name would smell as sweet.

*Romeo and Juliet*

Lord, what fools these mortals be!

*A Midsummer Night's Dream*

I'll put a girdle round the earth,
In forty minutes.

*A Midsummer Night's Dream*

If music be the food of love, play on.

*Twelfth Night*

But be not afraid of greatness: some are born great, some
achieve greatness, and some have greatness thrust upon
them.

*Twelfth Night*

Everyone can master a grief but he that has it.

*Much Ado About Nothing*

If all the year were playing holidays,
To sport would be as tedious as to work.

*King Henry IV Part I*

Out of this nettle, danger, we pluck this flower, safety.

*King Henry IV Part I*

Smooth runs the water where the brook is deep.

*King Henry VI*

Take honour from me, and my life is done.

*King Richard II*

Heat not a furnace for your foe so hot
That it do singe yourself.

*King Henry VIII*

To gild refined gold, to paint the lily,
To throw a perfume on the violet,
To smooth the ice, or add another hue
Unto the rainbow...
Is wasteful and ridiculous excess.

*King John*

... daffodils,
That come before the swallow dares, and take
The winds of March with beauty ...

*The Winter's Tale*

Let me not to the marriage of true minds
Admit impediments. Love is not love
Which alters when it alteration finds.

*Sonnets*

Shall I compare thee to a summer's day?
Thou art more lovely and more temperate.

*Sonnets*

William Shakespeare (1564 – 1616) was born at Stratford-upon-Avon and educated at the Free Grammar School. He left Stratford in about 1582 and went to London where he joined a company of players and soon became established as an actor and playwright. His plays brought him immediate fame. His output was prolific and his collected works as published today contain 37 plays, 2 long poems and 154 sonnets. The plays are divided into 17 comedies, 10 histories and 10 tragedies. He basked in the favour of Queen Elizabeth I and her successor, King James I, but eventually ceased to write and retired once again to Stratford-upon-Avon.

# George Bernard Shaw

You can always tell an old soldier by the inside of his holsters and cartridge boxes. The young ones carry pistols and cartridges: the old ones grub.

*Arms and the Man*

I'm only a beer teetotaller, not a champagne teetotaller.

*Candida*

A man is like a phonograph with half a dozen records. You soon get tired of them all.

*Getting Married*

Go anywhere in England, where there are natural, wholesome, contented, and really nice English people; and what do you always find? That the stables are the real centre of the household.

*Heartbreak House*

Nothing is ever done in this world until men are prepared to kill one another if it is not done.

*Major Barbara*

There are two tragedies in life. One is not to get your heart's desire. The other is to get it.

*Man and Superman*

Home is the girl's prison and the woman's workhouse.

*Man and Superman*

You think that you are Ann's suitor: that you are the pursuer and she the pursued. Fool: it is you who are the pursued, the marked-down quarry, the destined prey.

*Man and Superman*

Marriage is popular because it combines the maximum of temptation with the maximum of opportunity.

*Maxims for Revolutionists*

I occasionally swank a little because people like it; a modest man is such a nuisance.

*On Modesty, 7.3.1937*

A play that will not last forty years and be all the better for it is not worth writing.

*On the Theatre*

The British soldier can stand up to anything except the British War Office.

*The Devil's Disciple*

People are always blaming their circumstances for what they are. I do not believe in circumstances. The people who get on in this world are the people who get up and look for the circumstances they want, and if they cannot find them, make them.

Success covers a multitude of blunders.

If you cannot get rid of the family skeleton, you may as well make it dance.

George Bernard Shaw (1856–1950), the son of a civil servant, left Ireland and came to London, where he became a brilliant debater among the Fabians. He wrote five novels, then became a playwright and consequently met with great success. His comedy *Pygmalion* was written especially for Mrs Patrick Campbell, and his letters to the actress Ellen Terry are of great interest.

## Bishop Fulton Sheen

Each of us comes into life with fists closed, set for aggressiveness and acquisition. But when we abandon life our hands are open; there is nothing on earth we need, nothing the soul can take with it.

Bishop Fulton Sheen (1895–1979) was an American Roman Catholic prelate and auxiliary bishop of New York from 1951 to 1966. He achieved widespread influence through his radio *Catholic Hour* and television programmes.

## Percy Bysshe Shelley

Like winged stars the fire-flies flash and glance,
Pale in the open moonshine, but each one
Under the dark trees seems a little sun,
A meteor tamed: a fixed star gone astray
From the silver regions of the Milky Way

*To Maria Gisborne in England, from Italy*

Make me thy lyre, even as the forest is:
What if my leaves are falling like its own?

*Ode to the West Wind*


Hail to thee, blithe Spirit!
Bird thou never wert,
That from Heaven or near it,
Pourest thy full heart
In profuse strains of unpremeditated art.

*To a Skylark*


Teach me half the gladness
That thy brain must know,
Such harmonious madness
From my lips would flow
The world should listen then – as I am listening now.

*To a Skylark*


Percy Bysshe Shelley (1792–1822) was born at Field
Place, Sussex, went to Eton and later to Oxford, but with
his friend and fellow student James Hogg he was expelled
for being the author of a pamphlet entitled *The Necessity
of Atheism*. Shelley's *Alastor* was published in 1816. In
that same year he began his friendship with Byron, and
about this time he wrote his *Hymn to Intellectual Beauty*
and *Mont Blanc*. In 1818 Shelley left England for Italy,
where he translated Plato's *Symposium* and finished
*Rosalind and Helen*. In Rome, in 1819, he was stirred to
indignation by the political events in England, in particular the Peterloo affair, which persuaded him to write his
*Mask of Anarchy*, an indictment of Castlereagh's adminis-
tration. At the end of 1819 the Shelleys moved to Pisa
where he wrote some of his finest lyrics, including *Ode to
the West Wind*, *To a Skylark* and *The Cloud*. He was
drowned while sailing near Spezia, but just before his
death he wrote more of his beautiful lyrics and a number
of love poems inspired by Jane Williams.

119

## Richard Brinsley Sheridan

Mrs Candour:  I'll swear her colour is natural: I have seen it come and go.

Lady Teazle:  I dare swear you have ma'am: it goes off at night, and comes again in the morning.

*The School for Scandal*

The Right Honourable gentleman is indebted to his memory for his jests, and to his imagination for his facts.

*Replying to Mr Dundas in the House of Commons*

O Lord, sir, when a heroine goes mad she always goes into white satin.

*The Critic*

Madam, a circulating library in a town is as an evergreen tree of diabolical knowledge! It blossoms through the year! And depend on it, Mrs Malaprop, that they who are so fond of handling the leaves, will long for the fruit at last.

*The Rivals*

You write with ease, to show your breeding,
But easy writing's curst hard reading.

*Clio's Protest*

Richard Brinsley Sheridan (1751–1816) was the son of Thomas Sheridan, an actor and author. His comedy *The Rivals* was written when he was only twenty-three and acted at Covent Garden in 1775. He followed this with *St Patrick's Day* and *The Duenna*, and acquired Garrick's share in Drury Lane Theatre in 1776. There he produced *A Trip to Scarborough* and *The School for Scandal*, and his famous farce *The Critic*, which appeared in 1779.

## Jean Christian Sibelius

Pay no attention to what the critics say. A statue has never been erected in honour of a critic.

Jean Christian Sibelius (1865–1957) was a Finnish composer. His father wanted him to take up the law, but instead he studied the violin and composition at Helsingfors and went on to Berlin and Vienna. In Britain and the

USA he was recognised as a major composer and became known for his orchestral *En Saga* and *Karelia*, the tone poems *Finlandia* and *Night Ride and Sunrise*, the appealing *Valse Triste*, and seven symphonies.

## Samuel Smiles

The shortest way to do many things is to do only one thing at once.

We often discover what *will* do, by finding out what will not do; and probably he who never made a mistake never made a discovery.

*Self-Help*

A place for everything, and everything in its place.

*Thrift*

Samuel Smiles (1812–1904) was born at Haddington and educated at Haddington Grammar School and Edinburgh University. He became in turn a doctor, journalist, and secretary to railway companies, but he achieved fame with his *Life of George Stephenson* and the popular didactic work *Self-Help*, published in 1859.

## Logan Pearsall Smith

Thank heaven, the sun has gone in, and I don't have to go out and enjoy it.

*All Trivia: Last words*

There are two things to aim at in life: first, to get what you want; and, after that, to enjoy it. Only the wisest of mankind achieve the second.

*Afterthoughts: Life and Human Nature*

Logan Pearsall Smith (1865–1946), born in Philadelphia, was an essayist who spent most of his life in England. He was the author of *The Youth of Parnassus* (1895) and many other works, including *Songs and Sonnets* and *Milton and his Modern Critics* (1940).

## Sydney Smith

The further he went West the more convinced he felt that the Wise Men came from the East.

As the French say, there are three sexes – men, women, and clergymen.

*Lady Holland's 'Memoirs'*

I was just going to pray for you at St Paul's, but with no very lively hope of success.

*H. Pearson, 'The Smith of Smiths'*

Dame Partington ... was seen ... with mop and pattens ... vigorously pushing away the Atlantic Ocean. The Atlantic Ocean beat Mrs Partington.

*Peter Plymley's Letters*

The Reverend Sydney Smith (1771–1845), lived for some time in Edinburgh as tutor of Michael Hicks Beach, and became friendly with Francis, Lord Jeffrey, the Baron Brougham and Vaux, with whom he founded the *Edinburgh Review* in 1802. In 1807 he published the *Letters of Peter Plymley* in defence of Catholic emancipation.

## Edmund Spenser

Sweet Thames, run softly, till I end my song.

*Prothalamion*

At length they all to merry London came,
To merry London, my most kindly nurse,
That to me gave this life's first native source.

*Prothalamion*

Sleep after toil, port after stormy seas,
Ease after war, death after life does greatly please.

*The Faerie Queene: Book 1*

And all for love, and nothing for reward.

*The Faerie Queene: Book 2*

Edmund Spenser (1552–92) was born in London, educated at Cambridge, and then entered the service of the Earl of Leicester. In 1580 he became secretary to the Lord Deputy in Ireland and while at Kilcolman Castle completed the first three books of *The Faerie Queene*. Kilcolman Castle was burnt down by rebels and Spenser and his family narrowly escaped. The last six books of *The Faerie Queene* were lost, probably destroyed in the fire at the Castle.

## Madame de Staël

Politeness is the art of selecting among one's real thoughts.

Liberty is the only thing that at all times and in every country is in one's blood. Liberty and – what cannot be separated from it – love of one's country.

Life may often seem like a long shipwreck of which the debris are friendship, glory, and love. The shores of our existence are strewn with them.

Ann Louise Germaine de Staël (1766–1817), a French author, was born in Paris, the daughter of the financier Jacques Necker, and married the Baron de Staël-Holstein in 1785. An ardent advocate of political freedom, she was banished from Paris by Napoleon, but settled at Coppet on Lake Geneva and gathered around her men like A.W. von Schlegel, Byron and Benjamin Constant. Her most influential work was *De l'Allemagne*, which revealed to France the richness of German literature.

## Philip Dormer Stanhope

Be wiser than other people if you can, but do not tell them so.
*Letters to his Son, 19.11.1745*

An injury is much sooner forgotten than an insult.
*Letters to his Son, 9.10.1746*

I recommend you to take care of the minutes: for hours will take care of themselves.
*Letters to his Son, 6.11.1747*

Idleness is only the refuge of weak minds.
*Letters to his Son, 20.7.1749*

Philip Dormer Stanhope (1694–1773), fourth Earl of Chesterfield, was an opponent of Walpole and upon the latter's death became Lord Lieutenant of Ireland in 1745 and a Secretary of State in 1746. He was associated with Swift, Pope, and Bolingbroke and is remembered chiefly for his *Letters to his Son*.

## Stendhal

The better you know mankind, the more you are able to overlook the little shortcomings of your friends.

Nothing is less certain than success.

The world is full of people who can't bear being alone and to whom any remark, however uninteresting it may be, is better than nothing at all.

Heroes have intervals of fear, cowards moments of bravery, and virtuous women moments of weakness.

Stendhal (1783–1842) was the pseudonym of the French novelist Marie Henri Beyle. Born in Grenoble, he served in the ill-fated Russian campaign. Failing in his hopes of being a prefect, he lived in Italy from 1814, but suspicion of espionage drove him back to Paris, where he supported himself by literary hack-work. Balzac favourably reviewed his *La Chartreuse de Parme*, and from 1830 he was a member of the consular service.

## Robert Louis Stevenson

The cruellest lies are often told in silence.
*Virginibus Puerisque: El Dorado*
*of Intercourse*

For God's sake give me the young man who has brains enough to make a fool of himself.
*Virginibus Puerisque:*
*Crabbed Age and Youth*

There is no duty we so much underrate as the duty of being happy.
*Virginibus Puerisque: An*
*Apology for Idlers*

To travel hopefully is a better thing than to arrive, and the true success is to labour.

*Virginibus Puerisque: El Dorado*

Here lies one who meant well, tried a little, failed much...

*Across the Plains, A Christmas Sermon*

In winter I get up at night
And dress by yellow candle-light.
In summer quite the other way, –
I have to go to bed by day.

*A Child's Garden of Verses, Bed in Summer*

A child should always say what's true,
And speak when he is spoken to.
And behave mannerly at table:
At least as far as he is able.

*A Child's Garden of Verses, Whole Duty of Children*

Politics is perhaps the only profession for which no preparation is thought necessary.

Even if the doctor does not give you a year, even if he hesitates about a month, make one brave push and see what can be accomplished in a week.

Go, little book, and wish to all,
Flowers in the garden, meat in the hall,
A bin of wine, a spice of wit,
A house with lawns enclosing it,
A living river by the door,
A nightingale in the sycamore!

*Underwoods: 1. Envoy*

So long as we love we serve; so long as we are loved by others, I would almost say we are indispensable.

Keep your fears to yourself but share your courage.

Robert Louis Stevenson (1850–94) entered Edinburgh University in 1867 and studied engineering, but he soon abandoned it for the law. An illness of the lungs led to his frequent journeys in search of health, and his *Inland Voyage* described a canoe tour in Belgium and France.

His *Travels with a Donkey* followed the following year. Although very ill he contributed to many periodicals and wrote a number of essays, short stories, and fragments of travel and autobiography. He became famous because of his *Treasure Island*, *The Strange Case of Dr Jekyll and Mr Hyde*, *Kidnapped*, *Catriona*, *The Black Arrow* and *The Master of Ballantrae*. He also wrote some remarkable poetry, which was collected in *A Child's Garden of Verses* and *Underwoods*.

## Leopold Stokowski

It is not necessary to understand music;
It is only necessary that one enjoy it.

Leopold Stokowski (1887–1977) was an American conductor. Born in London of British and Polish parentage, he studied at the Royal College of Music and was conductor of the Cincinnati Symphony Orchestra between 1909 and 1912, and of the Philadelphia Orchestra from 1913 to 1936, becoming an American citizen in 1915. An outstanding experimentalist, he introduced much contemporary music into the United States and appeared in a number of films, including Walt Disney's *Fantasia*.

## Gladys Swarthout

A bright smile has compensated for many a vocal flaw in a concert.

Gladys Swarthout (1904–69) was an American opera singer. She also acted in a number of films, notably *Rose of the Rancho*, *Give us this Night*, *Champagne* and *Romance in the Dark*.

## Jonathan Swift

And he gave it for his opinion, that whoever could make two ears of corn or two blades of grass to grow upon a spot of ground where only one grew before, would deserve better of mankind, and do more essential service to his country than the whole race of politicians put together.

*Gulliver's Travels*

I have ever hated all nations, professions and communities, and all my love is towards individuals...

*Letter to Pope, 29.9.1725*

So, naturalists observe, a flea
Hath smaller fleas that on him prey;
And these have smaller fleas to bite 'em,
And so proceed *ad infinitum*.
Thus every poet, in his kind,
Is bit by him that comes behind.

*On Poetry*

The time is not remote when I
Must by the course of nature die:
When I foresee my special friends
Will try to find their private ends:
Though it is hardly understood
Which way my death can do them good...

... thus methinks I hear 'em speak:
'See, how the Dean begins to break,
Poor gentleman he droops apace,
You plainly find it in his face;
That old vertigo in his head
Will never leave him till he's dead...

Besides, his memory decays,
He recollects not what he says,
He cannot call his friends to mind,
Forgets the place where last he dined,
Plies you with stories o'er and o'er –
He's told them fifty times before.

*Verses on the Death of Doctor Swift by himself*

Jonathan Swift (1667–1745) was born in Dublin and educated at Kilkenny Grammar School. A cousin of Dryden, he was admitted to the household of Sir William Temple in Moor Park near Farnham, where he acted as Secretary. While there he wrote a number of Pindarics. Returning to Ireland he was ordained in 1694, but went back to Sir William and edited his correspondence. He also wrote *The Battle of the Books* and *A Tale of a Tub*.

Upon the death of Sir William, Swift went back to Ireland and was given a prebend in St Patrick's, Dublin. In 1713 he was made Dean of St Patrick's and from there he wrote the famous Drapier Letters. In 1726 he wrote *Gulliver's Travels*, which was really a satire on parties and statesmen, but soon it became a classic of children's literature. Nearly all Jonathan Swift's writings were published anonymously and it is possible that the £200 he received for *Gulliver's Travels* was the only payment he ever had.

## Algernon Charles Swinburne

Before the beginning of years
There came to the making of man
Time with a gift of tears,
Grief with a glass that ran.
Pleasure with pain for leaven,
Summer with flowers that fell.

*Atalanta in Calydon*

I have put my days and dreams out of mind,
Days that are over, dreams that are done.

*The Triumph of Time*

Change in a trice
The lilies and langours of virtue
For the raptures and roses of vice.

*Dolores*

Algernon Charles Swinburne (1837–1909) was educated at Eton and Balliol College, Oxford. In his early years he became friendly with Rossetti and his circle, but his first published volume attracted little attention. *Atalanta in Calydon* had choruses which revealed Swinburne's mastery of melodious verse, and this brought him celebrity. In 1867 he published *A Song of Italy* and in 1871 *Songs before Sunrise*. These were written during the struggle for Italian independence and showed Swinburne's political idealism.

## Tagore

God, the great giver, can open the whole universe to our gaze in the narrow space of a single lane.

Sir Rabindranath Tagore (1861–1941) was an Indian poet and a Nobel Prize-winner in 1913. His works are marked by deep religious feeling and a strong sense of the beauty of earth and sky in his native land, as well as his love of childhood. This is shown particularly in his poem *The Crescent Moon*. Tagore wrote mainly in Bengali, but he also wrote in English and translated into English some of his own Indian works.

## Sir Thomas Talfourd

'Tis a little thing
To give a cup of water; yet its draught
Of cool refreshment, drain'd by fever'd lips,
May give a shock of pleasure to the frame
More exquisite than when nectarean juice
Renews the life of joy in happiest hours.

*Ion*

Sir Thomas Noon Talfourd (1795–1854) was a judge and author but made little impression himself. He is principally remembered as the friend of Charles Lamb, whose *Letters* and *Memorials* he published in 1837 and 1848, although Charles Lamb died in 1834.

## Charles Maurice de Talleyrand

They have learnt nothing, and forgotten nothing.

*Attributed to Talleyrand by
the Chevalier du Pan, Jan
1796*

It is the beginning of the end.

*Remark to Napoleon after the
battle of Leipzig, 18.10.1813*

War is much too serious a thing to be left to military men.

You do not play whist, sir? Alas, what a sad old age you are preparing for yourself.

*When reproached for his
addiction to cards*

Black as the devil,
Hot as hell,
Pure as an angel,
Sweet as love.

*Talleyrand's recipe for coffee*

Charles Maurice de Talleyrand (1754–1838) was a French statesman. He was born in Paris and was a supporter of modern reform, but fled to the USA during the Terror of the French Revolution. He returned to France in 1796 and served as Foreign Minister under the Directory from 1778–9, continuing under Napoleon from 1799 to 1807. He represented France at the Congress of Vienna (1814–15), and was ambassador to London from 1830 to 1834.

## Jack Tanner

The shop steward is a little like an egg.
If you keep him in hot water long enough, he gets hard-boiled.

Jack (Frederick John Shirley) Tanner (1889–1965) was born in Whitstable. He was President of the Amalgamated Engineering Union from 1939–54, and was awarded the CBE in 1954. In 1943 he became Member of the TUC General Council, and was President from 1953–54.

## Alfred, Lord Tennyson

Their's not to make reply,
Their's not to reason why,
Their's but to do or die:
Into the valley of Death
Rode the six hundred.

*The Charge of the Light
Brigade*

I climb the hill: from end to end
Of all the landscape underneath,
I find no place that does not breathe
Some gracious memory of my friend.

*In Memoriam (of Arthur
Hallam)*

'Tis better to have loved and lost
Than never to have loved at all.
*In Memoriam (of Arthur Hallam)*

Kind hearts are more than coronets,
And simple faith than Norman blood.
*Lady Clara Vere de Vere*

Knowledge comes, but wisdom lingers.
*Locksley Hall*

In the Spring a young man's fancy lightly turns to
thoughts of love.
*Locksley Hall*

A lie which is half a truth is ever the blackest of lies,
A lie which is all a lie may be met and fought with
outright,
But a lie which is part a truth is a harder matter to fight.
*The Grandmother*

It is the little rift within the lute,
That by and by will make the music mute,
And ever widening slowly silence all.
*The Idylls of the King, The Passing of Arthur*

If thou shouldst never see my face again,
Pray for my soul. More things are wrought by prayer
Than this world dreams of. Wherefore, let thy voice
Rise like a fountain for me night and day.
*The Idylls of the King, The Passing of Arthur*

The mirror crack'd from side to side;
'The curse is come upon me' cried
The Lady of Shalott.
*The Lady of Shalott*

At Flores in the Azores Sir Richard Grenville lay,
And a pinnace, like a fluttered bird, came flying from far
away:
'Spanish ships of war at sea! we have sighted fifty-three!'
*The Revenge*

The gods themselves cannot recall their gifts.
*Tithonus*

There is sweet music here that softer falls
Than petals from blown roses on the grass,
Or night-dews on still waters between walls
Of shadowy granite, in a gleaming pass.

Here are cool mosses deep
And thro' the moss the ivies creep,
And in the stream the long-leaved flowers weep,
And from the craggy ledge the poppy hangs in sleep.

The Lotus blooms below the barren peak:
The Lotus blows by every winding creek:
All day the wind breathes low with mellower tone:
Thro' every hollow cave and alley lone.

*The Song of the Lotus-Eaters*

Alfred, first Baron Tennyson (1809–92) was educated at
Trinity College, Cambridge, where he became friendly
with A.H. Hallam. He won the chancellor's medal for
English verse in 1829 with a poem called *Timbuctoo*. In
1832 Tennyson travelled with Hallam on the Continent,
but Hallam died in 1833. Tennyson immediately began
*In Memoriam*, expressing grief for his dead friend. This
was followed by many poems and *The Idylls of the King*.

## William Makepeace Thackeray

There were three sailors of Bristol City
Who took a boat and went to sea.
But first with beef and captain's biscuits
And pickled pork they loaded she.
There was gorging Jack and guzzling Jimmy,
And the youngest he was little Billee.
Now when they got as far as the Equator
They'd nothing left but one split pea.

*Little Billee*

Says gorging Jim to guzzling Jacky,
We have no wittles, so we must eat *we*.

*Little Billee*

There's little Bill as is young and tender,
We're old and tough – so let's eat *he*.

*Little Billee*

William Makepeace Thackeray (1811–63) was educated at Charterhouse and at Trinity College, Cambridge. He studied little, and left in June 1830 without a degree after having made friends with Edward FitzGerald, Tennyson and others. He left England and settled in Paris in order to study drawing, but in 1837 he returned to England and contributed *The Yellowplush Correspondence* to *Fraser's Magazine*. He adopted the characters of George Savage Fitz-Boodle and Michael Angelo Titmarsh, and began to contribute to *Punch*. *Vanity Fair* appeared first in serial form, but Thackeray also lectured, his subjects being 'The English Humourists of the Eighteenth Century' and 'The Four Georges'.

## Margaret Thatcher

I've a woman's ability to stick to a job and get on with it when everyone else walks off and leaves it.
*16.2.1975*

Never in the history of human credit has so much been owed.
*12.10.1975*

If your only opportunity is to be equal, then it is not equality.
*28.11.1976*

I hope to be Prime Minister one day and I do not want there to be one street in Britain I cannot go down.
*1.5.1977*

Mrs Margaret Hilda Thatcher (1925–), was educated at Grantham High School and Somerville College, Oxford. A research chemist, she later became MP for Finchley and Parliamentary Secretary for the Ministry of Pensions and National Insurance. After being Chief Opposition Spokesman on Education and Secretary of State for Education and Science, she became Leader of the Conservative Party in 1975, and Prime Minister in May 1979.

## Dylan Thomas

In the sun that is young once only,
Time let me play and be
Golden in the mercy of his means.

*Fern Hill*

And green and golden I was huntsman and herdsman.

*Fern Hill*

In the sun born over and over,
I ran my heedless ways,
My wishes raced through the house high hay,
And nothing I cared ...

*Fern Hill*

The force that drives the water through the rocks
Drives my red blood.

*The Force that through the
Green fuse drives the Flower*

Nothing grows in our garden, only washing. And babies.

*Under Milk Wood*

Dylan Thomas (1914–53) was born in Swansea, the son
of the English master at the local school where he was
educated. Beginning as a reporter on the *South Wales
Evening Post*, he later became a journalist in London,
and published his volume *Eighteen Poems* in 1934. He
reached mastery of his medium in *Deaths and Entrances*
and *Under Milk Wood*, and his short stories entitled
*Portrait of the Artist as a Young Dog* are autobiographical.
He died in New York while on a series of reading and
lecture tours.

## James Thomson

Give a man a pipe he can smoke,
Give a man a book he can read;
And his home is bright with a calm delight,
Though the room be poor indeed.

*Gifts*

James Thomson (1834–82), the child of poor parents,
made friends with Charles Bradlaugh, the English free-
thinker and politician, wrote for the *National Reformer*,

and took an active part in the propaganda of free thought. His chief poem was *The City of Dreadful Night*. It was contributed to the *National Reformer* in 1874 and later re-published with other poems in 1880.

## H.D. Thoreau

I had three chairs in my house; one for solitude, two for friendship, three for society.

*Walden: Visitors*

The mass of men lead lives of quiet desperation.

*Walden: Economy*

Beware of all enterprises that require new clothes.

*Walden: Economy*

I never found the companion that was so companionable as solitude.

*Walden: Solitude*

Love your life, poor as it is. You may perhaps have some pleasant, thrilling, glorious hours, even in a poorhouse.

*Walden: Conclusion*

Some circumstantial evidence is very strong, as when you find a trout in the milk.

*Journal, 11.11.1854*

Henry David Thoreau (1817–62), the American writer and essayist, was born at Concord, Massachusetts, and educated at Harvard. A mystic, transcendentalist and natural philosopher, he rebelled against the Puritanism of New England and the materialistic values of modern society. He built himself a cabin by Walden Pond and lived there on practically nothing for two-and-a-half years.

## Leo Tolstoy

All happy families resemble each other, each unhappy family is unhappy in its own way.

*Anna Karenina*

Count Leo Nikolaevitch Tolstoy (1828–1910) was a Russian author, social reformer and religious mystic. He attended Kayan University, then joined the army, but left it after the siege of Sebastopol in 1855. Later he became a fanatical believer in non-violence. Tolstoy had great importance and amazing power, which spread his influence far beyond Russia and made him something of a prophet to many minds in the West. During the last few years of his life he shared the poor life of the peasants.

## Harry S. Truman

The White House is the finest jail in the world.
*On the United States of America*

It's a recession when your neighbour loses his job; it's a depression when you lose yours.
*On Industry*

Everybody has the right to express what he thinks. That, of course, lets the crackpots in. But if you cannot tell a crackpot when you see one, then you ought to be taken in.

Harry S. Truman (1884 – 1972) was an American statesman who was President between the years 1945–1953. As Democratic Vice-President, he took the office of President on the death of Franklin D. Roosevelt, and authorised the use of the first atomic bomb on Japan which devastated the City of Hiroshima, but was instrumental in ending the war against Japan. Truman implemented the Marshall Plan to aid the recovery of post-war Europe and the 'Truman Doctrine'.

## Mark Twain

There's plenty of boys that will come hankering and gruvvelling around when you've got an apple, and beg the core off you ...
*Tom Sawyer Abroad*

The report of my death was an exaggeration.
*Cable from Europe to the Associated Press*

In Boston they ask, How much does he know? In New York, How much is he worth? In Philadelphia, Who were his parents?

*What Paul Bourget thinks of us*

A classic is something that everybody wants to have read and nobody wants to read.

*Speeches: The Disappearance
of Literature*

Cauliflower is nothing but cabbage with a college education.

*Pudd'nhead Wilson's Calendar*

They spell it Vinci and pronounce it Vinchy: foreigners always spell better than they pronounce.

*The Innocents Abroad*

Mark Twain (Samuel Langhorne Clemens, 1835–1910) first came into prominence as a writer with his *Jim Smiley and his Jumping Frog*. His best-known works are *The Innocents Abroad*, *The Adventures of Tom Sawyer* and *The Adventures of Huckleberry Finn*. He also wrote *A Connecticut Yankee in King Arthur's Court* in 1889.

## Peter Ustinov

The sound of laughter has always seemed to me the most civilized music in the universe.

*from 'Dear Me'*

To be gentle, tolerant, wise and reasonable requires a goodly portion of toughness.

Peter Ustinov (1921–) is a British actor-dramatist. Born in London, he has ventured into almost every aspect of film and theatre life. He has written plays, being sometimes author, director, producer and principal actor in them. In 1963 he became joint director of the Nottingham Playhouse.

## Sir John Vanbrugh

Good manners and soft words have brought many a difficult thing to pass.

Sir John Vanbrugh (1664 – 1726) was an English dramatist and architect. Born in London, he designed Blenheim Palace and the first Haymarket Theatre, London.

## Ralph Vaughan-Williams

My advice to all who want to attend a lecture on music is don't. Go to a concert instead.

Ralph Vaughan-Williams (1872–1958) was a British composer who was born in Gloucester and studied at Cambridge and the Royal College of Music. He learnt much from Max Bruch in Berlin and Ravel in Paris. He wrote a number of symphonies, and in 1951 his operatic morality *The Pilgrim's Progress* was performed for the Festival of Britain. Later works included *Sinfonia Antarctica* which was used in the film *Scott of the Antarctic*, and a ninth symphony. He received the OM in 1935.

## Alfred de Vigny

Silence alone is great; all else is feebleness.
*La Mort du Loup*

Alfred de Vigny (1797–1863) was a French poet. Born at Loches, he joined the army at sixteen and had twelve years' service. His first volume of poems appeared in 1822 and was followed by his prose romance *Cinq Mars*. His drama *Chatterton* showed his interest in England where he lived for some years, after marrying an Englishwoman in 1828.

## Publius Vergilius Maro Virgil

We cannot all do all things.
*Eclogues*

Now the Virgin returns; now Saturn is King again and a new and better race descends from on high.
*Eclogues*

The last age, heralded in Cumean song, is come, and the great march of the centuries begins anew.
*Eclogues*

Happy he who has been able to learn the causes of things.
*Georgics*

But meanwhile ... time is flying that cannot be recalled.
*Georgics*

Not ignorant of ill do I learn to aid the wretched.
*Aeneid*

Even here, virtue hath her rewards, and mortality her tears; even here, the woes of man touch the heart of man.
*Aeneid*

Roman, be this thy care – these thine arts – to bear dominion over the nations and to impose the law of peace, to spare the humbled and to war down the proud.
*Aeneid*

I fear the Greeks even when they bring gifts.
*Aeneid*

From one piece of villainy judge them all.
*Aeneid*

A fickle and changeable thing is woman ever.
*Aeneid*

Virgil (Publius Vergilius Maro, 70–19BC), the Roman poet, was born near Mantua and eulogized his own yeoman class in his poems. He was patronized by Maecenas and his *Eclogues* (ten pastoral poems) appeared in 37BC. These were followed in 30BC by the *Georgics*, confirming him as the chief poet of the age. The last years of his life were spent in composing the *Aeneid*, an epic poem in twelve books intended to glorify the Julian dynasty, whose head was Augustus. An apparent forecast of the birth of Christ in the fourth *Eclogue* led to his acceptance as an 'honorary' Christian by the medieval Church and in popular legend he became a powerful magician.

## Voltaire

If God did not exist, it would be necessary to invent him.
*Letters: To the Author of the
Book of the Three Imposters*

In this country [England] it is good to kill an admiral
from time to time, to encourage the others.
*Candide, In allusion to the
shooting of Admiral Byng*

This agglomeration which was called and which still calls
itself the Holy Roman Empire was neither holy, nor
Roman, nor an Empire.

I disapprove of what you say, but I will defend to the
death your right to say it.
*Attributed*

Voltaire (1694–1778) was the pseudonym of the French
writer François-Marie Arouet. Born in Paris, the son of a
notary, he adopted his pseudonym when he had already
started writing poetry while still at his Jesuit seminary.
His early essay offended the authorities and during the
years 1716–26 he was twice imprisoned in the Bastille
and thrice exiled from the capital for having written
libellous political verse. Later in life he was at the Court
of Frederick the Great who had long admired him, but
the association ended in deep enmity and Voltaire established himself near Geneva. He is remembered for a
number of works, but particularly for *Candide* and the
tragedy *Irene*.

## Lewis Wallace

Beauty is altogether in the eye of the beholder.
*The Prince of India*

Lewis Wallace (1827–1905) was a US general and novelist. He served in the Mexican and Civil Wars and
subsequently became governor of New Mexico and
minister to Turkey. He wrote the historical novels *The
Fair God* and *Ben-Hur*.

# Horace Walpole

Here lies Fred
Who was alive and is dead:
Had it been his father,
I had much rather.
Had it been his brother,
Still better than another:
Had it been his sister,
No-one would have missed her.

Had it been the whole generation,
Still better for the nation;
But since 'tis only Fred,
Who was alive and is dead
There's no more to be said.

*Written after the death of*
*Frederick,*
*Prince of Wales in 1751*

Strawberry Hill is a little plaything house that I got out of
Mrs Chenevix's shop, and is the prettiest bauble you ever
saw. It is set in enamelled meadows, with filigree hedges.

*Letters: To Conway, 8 June*
*1747*

Horace Walpole (1717–97) was the fourth son of Sir
Robert Walpole. He travelled in France and Italy with
Thomas Gray and later he settled at Strawberry Hill,
Twickenham, where he established a printing press.
Here he printed Gray's two Pindaric odes and his own
*Anecdotes of Painting in England.* In 1764 he published
his Gothic story *The Castle of Otranto*, but it is on his
*Letters* that Walpole's literary reputation rests. They are
said to be remarkable both for their charm and their
autobiographical, social and political interest.

# Izaak Walton

Look to your health; if you have it, praise God, and value
it next to a good conscience; for health is the second
blessing that we mortals are capable of; a blessing that
money cannot buy.

*Compleat Angler,*
*Part 1 Ch 21*

Izaak Walton (1593 – 1683) was an English author born in Stafford. He settled in London as an ironmonger and wrote short biographies of his friends Donne, Hooker, Sir Henry Wotton and George Herbert. He is well-known for his book *The Compleat Angler,* the location of which was the River Lea near London.

## Isaac Watts

Let dogs delight to bark and bite,
For God hath made them so:
Let bears and lions growl and fight,
For 'tis their nature too.

But, children, you should never let
Such angry passions rise:
Your little hands were never made
To tear each other's eyes.

*Divine Songs for Children,*
*Against Quarrelling*

*Isaac Watts (1674 –1748) was the son of a Nonconformist* schoolmaster and is remembered as the author of *Divine Songs for Children.* He also wrote a number of hymns, some of which have obtained a wide popularity. These *include O God, our help in ages past* and *When I survey the wondrous cross.*

## Evelyn Waugh

The great charm in argument is really finding one's own opinion, not other people's.

Evelyn Arthur St John Waugh (1903 – 66) was a British novelist. Educated at Oxford, he later published studies of Edmund Campion and Ronald Knox. His novels achieved fame, particularly *The Loved One* and *Brides-head Revisited* which was recently televised.

# Duke of Wellington

I don't know what effect these men will have upon the enemy, but, by God, they terrify me.

*On a draft of troops sent to him in Spain, 1809*

All the business of war, and indeed all the business of life, is to endeavour to find out what you don't know by what you do; that's what I called 'guessing what was at the other side of the hill'.

*Croker Papers*

It has been a damned serious business – Blücher and I have lost 30,000 men.

*Creevey Papers*

It has been a damned nice thing – the nearest run thing you ever saw in your life ... By God! I don't think it would have done if I had not been there.

*Creevey Papers*

Arthur Wellesley (1769–1852), first Duke of Wellington, was born in Ireland and educated at Eton. He then entered the army and was sent to India. There he achieved victories over the Mahrattas at Assaye and Argaum, and negotiated a Peace which earned him a knighthood. After establishing his reputation in the Peninsular War he defeated the French at Vimeiro, expelled the French from Spain, and was made Duke of Wellington. Following Napoleon's escape from Elba, he defeated him at Quatre-Bras and at Waterloo.

# H.G. Wells

I was thinking jest what a Rum Go everything is.

*Kipps*

The world may discover that all its common interests are being managed by one concern ...

*A Short History of the World*

Herbert George Wells (1866–1946) was the son of a professional cricketer. He took a degree at the Royal College of Science, South Kensington, taught for some years, then made his name in science fiction with such publications as *The Time Machine, The Invisible Man* and *The War of the Worlds*. Later he wrote more stories, including *Kipps, The History of Mr. Polly* and *The Shape of Things to Come*.

## Orson Wells

In Italy for thirty years under the Borgias they had warfare, terror, murder, bloodshed, but they produced Michelangelo, Leonardo da Vinci, and the Renaissance. In Switzerland, they had brotherly love, they had five hundred years of democracy and peace. And what did that produce? The cuckoo-clock.

> *(Orson Wells added these words to the Graham Greene–Carol Reed script of 'The Third Man')*

Orson Wells (1915–) is known as an ebullient actor-writer-producer-director with stage and radio experience. In 1938 he panicked the whole of America with a vivid radio version of *The War of the Worlds*, and in 1970 he was awarded an Academy Award for 'supreme artistry and versatility in the creation of motion pictures'.

## John Wesley

Do all the good you can,
By all the means you can,
In all the ways you can,
In all the places you can,
At all the times you can,
To all the people you can,
As long as ever you can.

> *Methodist Rule of Conduct*

John Wesley (1703 – 91) was the brother of Charles Wesley, the founder of a 'methodist' society of pious young men and composer of many hymns including *Jesu, lover of my soul*. John Wesley was a man of real and deep learning. He published twenty-three collections of hymns as well as his collected prose *Works*, and his *Journal* which is remarkable for its pathos, humour and observation of mankind. Methodism was a movement of reaction against the apathy of the Church of England that prevailed in the early part of the eighteenth century.

# Gilbert White

Many horses, though quiet with company, will not stay one minute in a field by themselves; the strongest fences cannot restrain them. My neighbour's horse will not only not stay by himself abroad, but he will not bear to be alone in a strange stable without discovering the utmost impatience, and endeavouring to break the rack and manger with his fore feet.

*Sociable Animals, The*
*Natural History of Selborne*

Gilbert White (1720–93), the English naturalist, was born at Selborne, Hampshire. He took orders in 1747 and in 1751 retired to his birthplace where he wrote *Natural History and Antiquities of Selborne* which has become a classic. His home, 'The Wakes', was opened as a museum and library in 1955.

# Ella Wheeler Wilcox

Laugh and the world laughs with you,
Weep, and you weep alone.
For the sad old earth must borrow its mirth
But has trouble enough of its own.

*Solitude*

Have you heard of the terrible family They,
And the dreadful venomous things They say?
Why, half of the gossip under the sun
If you trace it back you will find begun
In that wretched house of They.

Ella Wheeler Wilcox (1850–1919) was an American poet and journalist. She was described as 'the most popular poet of either sex and of any age read by thousands who never open Shakespeare'. She began to publish poems in 1872 and her last volume, *Poems of Affection*, was published posthumously.

## Oscar Wilde

To lose one parent, Mr Worthing, may be regarded as a misfortune; to lose both looks like carelessness.

*The Importance of Being Earnest*

I have invented an invaluable permanent invalid called Bunbury, in order that I may be able to go down into the country whenever I choose.

*The Importance of Being Earnest*

All women become like their mothers. That is their tragedy. No man does. That's his.

*The Importance of Being Earnest*

I never saw a man who looked
With such a wistful eye
Upon that little tent of blue
Which prisoners call the sky.

*The Ballad of Reading Gaol*

Oscar Fingal O'Flahertie Wills Wilde (1854 – 1900) was a poet and dramatist. Educated at Trinity College, Dublin, and Magdalen College, Oxford, he gained a reputation as founder of an aesthetic cult. This was caricatured in Gilbert and Sullivan's comic opera *Patience*. His first volume, *Poems*, was followed by several works of fiction including *The Picture of Dorian Gray*. Then came *Lady Windermere's Fan*, *A Woman of No Importance* and *The Importance of Being Earnest*. The most remarkable of his works are said to be *The Ballad of Reading Gaol* and *De Profundis*, both being written about his own imprisonment.

## John Wilmot, Earl of Rochester

Were I (who to my cost already am
One of those strange, prodigious creatures, man)
A spirit free to choose, for my own share,
What case of flesh and blood I pleased to wear,
I'd be a dog, a monkey or a bear,
Or anything but that vain animal
Who is so proud of being rational.

*Homo Sapiens*

John Wilmot, Earl of Rochester (1647–80), was a British poet who showed gallantry at sea in the Second Dutch War. He spent much of his time at Court where he established a reputation for debauchery. His poems include many graceful lyrics and some powerful satires, the best of which is said to be *A Satire Against Mankind*.

## Harold Wilson

If I had the choice between smoked salmon and tinned salmon, I'd have it tinned. With vinegar.

*11.11.1962*

One man's pay increase is another man's price increase.

*11.1.1970*

If you buy land on which is a slagheap 120 feet high and it costs £100,000 to remove it, that is not speculation but land reclamation.

*7.4.1974*

The monarchy is a labour-intensive industry.

*13.2.1977*

I do not think any Minister should shelter behind his civil servants.

*6.3.1977*

Sir Harold Wilson (1916–) was Leader of the Labour Party in 1968–76, and Prime Minister in 1964–70 and 1974–76. He entered Parliament in 1945 as member for Ormskirk, and was elected for Huyton in 1950. As Prime Minister in 1964 he faced a formidable balance of payments deficit, and in 1974 found himself head of the first minority government since 1929. In an election in October 1974 he secured the narrowest overall majority in any election in recent history. Sir Harold Wilson resigned his office as Prime Minister in 1976.

## William Wordsworth

I travelled among unknown men
In lands beyond the sea;
Nor, England! did I know till then
What love I bore to thee.

*I Travelled among Unknown Men*

I wandered lonely as a cloud
That floats on high o'er vales and hills,
When all at once I saw a crowd,
A host, of golden daffodils;
Beside the lake, beneath the trees,
Fluttering and dancing in the breeze.

*I Wandered Lonely as a Cloud*

Up! up! my friend, and quit your books;
Or surely you'll grow double:

Come forth into the light of things,
Let Nature be your teacher.

One impulse from a vernal wood
May teach you more of man,
Of moral evil and of good,
Than all the sages can.

*The Tables Turned*

That best portion of a good man's life,
His little, nameless, unremembered acts
Of kindness and of love.

... The sounding cataract
Haunted me like a passion:

... I have learned
To look on nature, not as in the hour
Of thoughtless youth; but hearing often-times
The still, sad music of humanity.

*Lines composed a few miles
above Tintern Abbey*

This City now doth, like a garment, wear
The beauty of the morning.

*Sonnet composed upon Westminster Bridge*

Milton! thou should'st be living at this hour:
England hath need of thee; she is a fen
Of stagnant waters.

*Sonnet: London, 1802*

We must be free or die, who speak the tongue
That Shakespeare spake; the faith and morals hold
Which Milton held.

*Sonnet: It is not to be thought of*

William Wordsworth (1770–1850) was educated at the
grammar school at Hawkshead and St John's College,
Cambridge, and left the University without distinction.
In 1790 he went on a walking tour of France, the Alps
and Italy. Returning to France in 1791 he spent a year
there. The revolutionary movement was then at its height
and impressed him greatly. He fell in love with the
daughter of a French surgeon, and their story is told in
*Vaudracour and Julia*.

The French Revolution was followed by the English
declaration of war and 'The Terror', and Wordsworth's
republican enthusiasm gave place to a period of pessi-
mism. This manifested itself in his tragedy *The Borderers*
which was written in 1795/6. Wordsworth made the
acquaintance of S.T. Coleridge, and a long-enduring
friendship developed between them. Together they published *Lyrical Ballads* which marked a revival in English
poetry. In 1843 Wordsworth succeeded Southey as poet
laureate.

## Sir Henry Wotton

How happy is he born and taught
That serveth not another's will;
Whose armour is his honest thought,
And simple truth his utmost skill.

*Character of a Happy Life*

You meaner beauties of the night,
That poorly satisfy our eyes,
More by your number, than your light;
You common people of the skies,
What are you, when the moon shall rise?

*On His Mistress, the Queen of
Bohemia*

An ambassador is an honest man sent to lie abroad for the good of his country.

*Written in a friend's album*

Sir Henry Wotton (1568 – 1639) became agent and secretary to the Earl of Essex in 1595, and was employed by him in collecting foreign intelligence. He was involved in various diplomatic missions from 1604 to 1624. A collection of his poetical and other writings containing his famous work *Character of a Happy Life* and *On His Mistress, the Queen of Bohemia* was published in 1651. His *Life* was written by Izaak Walton in 1670.

## Xerxes

My men have become women, and my women men.

*When Queen Artemisia's ship sank another at Salamis, 480BC*

Xerxes, King of Persia (519?– 465BC) was the son of Darius I. He invaded Greece and overcame the resistance of Leonidas at Thermopylae, but was defeated at Salamis in 480BC. He is the King Ahasuerus of the Book of Esther.

## William Butler Yeats

... The land of faery,
Where nobody gets old and godly and grave,
Where nobody gets old and crafty and wise,
Where nobody gets old and bitter of tongue.

*The Land of Heart's Desire*

Had I the heavens' embroidered cloths,
Enwrought with golden and silver light.

*He wishes for the Cloths of Heaven*

I have spread my dreams under your feet;
Tread softly, because you tread on my dreams.

*He wishes for the Cloths of Heaven*

When you are old and grey and full of sleep,
And nodding by the fire, take down this book.

*When you are Old*

She bid me take life easy, as the grass grows on the weirs;
But I was young and foolish, and now am full of tears.
*Down by the Salley Gardens*


I will arise and go now, and go to Innisfree,
And a small cabin build there, of clay and wattles made:
Nine bean-rows will I have there, a hive for the honey-
bee.
And live alone in the bee-loud glade.
*The Lake Isle of Innisfree*


When I play on my fiddle in Dooney
Folk dance like a wave of the sea.
*The Fiddler of Dooney*


William Butler Yeats (1865–1939) was born in Dublin
and studied at the School of Art there. He developed an
interest in mystic religion and the supernatural, but at
the age of 21 he abandoned art as a profession and took to
writing, editing *The Poems of William Blake*, *The Works
of William Blake* and *The Poems of Spenser*. As a nationalist he applied himself to the creation of an Irish national
theatre, and with the help of Lady Gregory and others
partly achieved this ambition when his play *The Countess
Cathleen* was acted in Dublin.

Yeats's early study of Irish lore and legends resulted in
*Fairy and Folk Tales of the Irish Peasantry*, *The Celtic
Twilight* and *The Secret Rose*.

Under the influence of his wife and her 'communica-
tors', Yeats wrote many works and he was awarded the
Nobel Prize for Literature in 1923. He also published
collections of essays and edited many books, the most
important being *The Oxford Book of Modern Verse* which
was published in 1936. He wrote fine letters, and five
major collections have been made.


## Edward Young

Tir'd Nature's sweet restorer, balmy sleep!
He, like the world, his ready visit pays
Where fortune smiles; the wretched he forsakes.
*Night Thoughts*

Night, sable goddess! from her ebon throne
In rayless majesty, now stretches forth
Her leaden sceptre o'er a slumb'ring world.

*Night Thoughts*

Procrastination is the thief of time.

*Night Thoughts*

At thirty man suspects himself a fool;
Knows it at forty, and reforms his plan;
At fifty chides his infamous delay,
Pushes his prudent purpose to resolve;
In all the magnanimity of thought
Resolves; and re-resolves; then dies the same.

*Night Thoughts*

Some for renown, on scraps of learning dote,
And think they grow immortal as they quote.

*Love of Fame*

Edward young (1683–1765) took orders and became
rector of Welwyn in 1730, where he spent the remainder
of his long life, but he never received the ecclesiastical
promotion to which many of his contemporaries thought
him entitled.

His literary work includes *Busiris*, a tragedy of violence
and ungoverned passion, and *The Revenge*, another tragedy, but he also published a series of satires under the
title *The Universal Passion – the Love of Fame*, which were
much admired. He is, however, principally remebered
for *The Complaint or Night Thoughts on Life, Death and
Immortality*, which became very popular immediately it
was published (1742–5).

## Israel Zangwill

America is God's Crucible, the great Melting-Pot where
all the races of Europe are melting and reforming! ... God
is making the American.

*The Melting Pot, Act I*

Scratch the Christian and you find the pagain – spoiled.

*The Children of the Ghetto*

Israel Zangwill (1864 – 1926) was a Jewish writer, born in London of poor parents. He studied at London University and became famous for his *Children of the Ghetto* which was written at the request of the Jewish Publication Society of America for a story depicting Jewish life among the poorer classes. He wrote novels, plays and pamphlets, made several successful lecture tours in America, and was interested in the Zionist movement.

## Emile Zola

J'accuse – I accuse.

*Title of an open letter to the President of France in connection with the Dreyfus case, 13 January 1898*

Emile Edouard Charles Antoine Zola (1840 – 1902) was a French author, born in Paris. He left school early and engaged in journalism but with little success. Showing greater aptitude for story-telling, he wrote a collection of charming tales which were published under the title *Contes a' Ninon* and followed this with *L'Assommoir* which dealt with drunkenness and created a sensation. Most of his stories are very unconventional, but the exception is an idyllic tale called 'Le Rêve'.

In 1898 he successfully took up the cause of Captain Dreyfus, a French soldier accused of selling documents of value to the German Government. Because of Zola's intervention Dreyfus was pardoned, restored to the army, and later made an officer of the Legion of Honour.

# Acknowledgements and Sources

Boscombe (Bournemouth) Reference Library
Bournemouth Central Reference Library
Harpenden (Herts) Reference Library
New Milton (Hants) Reference Library
Winton (Bournemouth) Reference Library

*Collins' Dictionary of People and Places*
*Concise Oxford Dictionary of English Literature*
*Concise Oxford Dictionary of Quotations*
*Everyman's Dictionary of Quotations and Proverbs*
*Family Word Finder*
*Gilbert Harding's Book of Happiness*
*Hutchinson's New Twentieth Century Encyclopaedia*
*International Who's Who*
*New Oxford Book of English Verse 1250 – 1950*
*Pear's Cyclopaedia*
*Quote – Unquote* (Nigel Rees)
*Reader's Digest Library*
*Sayings of the Seventies* Colin Cross
*Sayings of the Week* Valerie Ferguson
*The Book of a Thousand Poems*
*Who's Who*
*Who Was Who*

# Index of Authors

156

157